THE PRUITT APPROACH
A Coyote Mentality

THE PRUITT APPROACH

A Coyote Mentality

A Book of Quotes

*To Michael
From Dad
Christmas 2016*

DAVID W. PRUITT

BROWN BOOKS
PUBLISHING GROUP

© 2015 David W. Pruitt

All rights reserved. No part of this book may be used or reproduced in any manner without written permission except in the case of brief quotations embodied in critical articles or reviews.

The Pruitt Approach— A Coyote Mentality
A Book of Quotes

Brown Books Publishing Group
16250 Knoll Trail Drive, Suite 205
Dallas, Texas 75248
www.BrownBooks.com
(972) 381-0009

A New Era in Publishing™

ISBN 978-1-61254-210-2 (HC)
978-1-61254-211-9 (PB)
LCCN 2015939381

Printed in the United States
10 9 8 7 6 5 4 3 2 1

Cover photograph is of electric lines owned by Cap Rock Energy, now Sharyland Utilities, LLP (a "wires" company), whose chairman, CEO, and president was David W. Pruitt.

(1915-2003)

To my father, Marion Manoah Pruitt.

Daddy was the best person I've ever known.

My only hero!

Contents

Foreword ix
Foreword xiii
Author's Note xv
    Friendship 1
    Spirituality 7
    Inspiration 21
    Vision 47
    Government 63
    Failure 73
    Fear 81
    Change 85
    Business 91
    Perseverance 109
    Success 117
    Leadership 133
    Motivation 143
    Humor 163
    Attitude 191
    Texas 209
    Love 219
Appendix 221
Index 225
About the Author 245

Foreword

David W. Pruitt is the kind of person that you meet only once in a lifetime. David is a throwback to the early entrepreneurs who helped make this country great. It is my distinct pleasure to have known him all of my life and especially to have known him as my boss, mentor, and friend for over twenty-five years.

David spent most of his adult life building companies and making them better for the employees, the customers, and the owners. He started in the electric cooperative world, and because he was a visionary and aggressive in trying to improve these companies, he often ran afoul of the very non-progressive good old boy political organizations that run the electric cooperatives in the United States. Nevertheless, David was not satisfied with merely managing the company, sitting back quietly, drawing a good salary, and not making waves so that his life would be easy and rewarding. To the contrary, he did what he knew was right for the customers, employees, and owners, and he set about to make changes, even when these actions caused him a lot of pain, heartache, and criticism personally.

David didn't start Cap Rock Electric Cooperative, but he made it into the successful company it became. When David took over as manager, it was a small rural electric cooperative which had high rates, hundreds of miles of lines, few customers, bad service, employees who made very little money, and old and dilapidated equipment. In a few years, he had raised employees' salaries, instilled pride in the employees (most of whom had to have second jobs in order to survive, prior to David's taking over), bought updated equipment, and instituted programs to upgrade the system, thereby improving reliability—all without raising rates.

The Pruitt Approach—A Coyote Mentality

Not satisfied with the status quo, under David's leadership, Cap Rock became the first electric cooperative in the US that paid off its loans from the Rural Electrification Association (REA) at a 50 percent discount. With David as the CEO, Cap Rock became the first electric cooperative in the US to convert to an investor-owned corporation, and it also became the first electric cooperative to become a public company, when it became listed on the American Stock Exchange. Under its new name, Cap Rock Energy, the company's stock rose to unprecedented heights. Its current and former members received payment in cash or stock (their choice) for their equity in the company, and the rates were among the lowest in the state. If the company had remained a cooperative, there was no law that required that the equity owners ever receive payment for their equity.

A few years later, David's tenacity led to the sale of Cap Rock to a private equity firm. Although Cap Rock was the smallest company the private equity firm had ever purchased, David's business savvy led to the former members, who had taken shares in the company as payment for their equity, more than doubling their money. This sale of a utility to a private equity firm was a blueprint later used by very large companies, such as TXU, Texas's largest electric utility, which sold to private equity firms. David Pruitt is a true pioneer and entrepreneur. All these firsts are not easy, however. Some say that when you are first, you take lots of arrows in the front and in the back. David took more than his share, and most people would have melted under the pressure and quit, but not David. He successfully pressed forward, and the company rewarded its owners, its employees, its management, and its customers. The company subsequently sold to another utility company and is well on its way to becoming one of the largest electric utilities in the state of Texas. This would not be the case if not for David Pruitt's vision and his never-give-up attitude.

This collection of quotes from a person like David should be helpful and an inspiration to all who read it. It is an insight to the quotes that inspired and motivated a person who accomplished great things. From my personal experience, I am familiar with many quotes he originated and lived by. He was my boss for over twelve years, my mentor, my hero, and my friend.

When David hired me, I was a good lawyer who had accomplished some good things in the courtroom. I had some skills, but David taught me how to be a successful lawyer. He mentored me and taught me that it is much more important to get things done and get things done promptly than taking more time to try to get things perfectly. He taught me to push matters and try to get done what needs to be done, even if everything, including legal precedent, seems to be against you. He taught me that a good general counsel does not worry about wordsmithing and that if you do not worry about looking smart or trying to make sure people do not think you are not smart, you can get things accomplished that you thought were not possible, and you will win more than you lose.

David accomplished so many things, and I am honored to have been a part of many of those. One of his quotes that he told me early on is still taped by the phone in my office: "Don't be reasonable." The other quote he often told me was "The rules do not apply to us." His purpose, I now know, was to inspire me not to deal with matters in the usual way and not to let people convince me that if we were reasonable, we wouldn't take some action. He also wanted me to realize that sometimes you have to make your own rules in order to accomplish things that everyone says cannot be done. If you play by other people's rules, you will not get it done. If you do not follow the rules, and make your own, sometimes you can accomplish great things.

Please enjoy this collection of quotes. It will give you some insight to one of the greatest entrepreneurs in the last thirty years, a man who accomplished many things that people laughed at and said could not be done. He did them. I hope this book inspires those who have those qualities and want to accomplish things others say cannot be done.

Ronnie Lyon, J D, Esq.

Former Executive Vice President & General Counsel, Cap Rock Energy

Foreword

When I heard my good ole boy of a friend, David Pruitt, was publishing a book of quotes, I got pretty jazzed. When he asked me to say a few words about him, I was honored to do so, especially in the context of a book of his favorite quotes. I have travelled with "Pruitt"—that is all I call him—all over the world, done business with him, "lawyered" for him, and seen him at and from every angle for nearly twenty years. No one I have met before or since got to the heart of a matter quicker than Pruitt, and he would tie a bow around his conclusions with a quote or a quip.

There is a great quote that basically says, "Wouldn't it be nice if God had given us the gift that we could see ourselves as others see us?" Pruitt may be one of the most self-aware people I have ever met, and seeing himself as simply and clearly as he does puts him in a position to see you and the simplicity of situations. Simplicity in an age of social media, international tension, intense business cycles, and general uncertainty is a tremendous gift. I remember, for example, being in a CEO Club meeting with Pruitt in Paris, France. There was a fellow CEO describing in minute detail the battle he was waging with his investors and partners. It was explanation of the Series A shareholder vs. Series B, Series B courting the bank, and this CEO's uncertain future. Pruitt didn't hesitate when it was his turn to give advice. He said, "Well, I suggest you start stealing everything you can. And I would start with the pencils." Now, we all got it immediately. He didn't literally mean to steal the pencils tomorrow. What Pruitt was saying was that in an environment like what the CEO described, everybody was already grabbing clients, positioning themselves for the after, and basically stealing already. With one quote, Pruitt told the guy what he needed to do—look out for yourself; the company is dead.

In my travels with Pruitt, he never met someone who didn't immediately become a friend. His charisma, magnetism, and sincere love for others show in his immediate engagement with them. It really didn't matter what language they spoke. Pruitt speaks English, but a severe form of the Midland dialect. I recall being in Chester, England, with Pruitt while he engaged a hackneyed Brit. I couldn't understand either one, but somehow they understood each other.

One of my fond memories is when my business partner and I drove down to Midland for one of Pruitt's big birthdays. We bought him a Remington. The bucking bronco. In the business world Pruitt rode in, nobody was more tenacious and could handle a wild business ride better than he could. And that tenacity was essential to his business success.

As you read his quotes, listen carefully. If Pruitt says something, you know it's important. And by golly, he cares about you whether he has met you or not, and he is sharing these because they kept him on the bronco and helped him succeed. Without a doubt, getting to the heart of the matter is what a quote helps us do. I hope you know David and know his unique voice and hear that voice as you read his quotes. If so, you may have to read the quote more than once. For me, even after twenty years I have to say, "Pruitt, say that again."

Steven Cash Nickerson

President PDS Tech;
Attorney Licensed in
Seven states

Author's Note

This book contains a collection of quotes I have gathered over the last thirty-plus years. Most reflect my attitude about life or thoughts at the time. Some of the quotes I thought were funny. Some inspired or challenged me throughout my business and career and also just life in general. My hope is at least a few will be enjoyable to you.

Thanks for taking time to read my collection.

Enjoy!

FRIENDSHIP

MOHAMMED ALI

Friendship is the hardest thing in the world to explain. It's not something you learn in school. But if you haven't learned the meaning of friendship, you really haven't learned anything!

THANK YOU FRIEND

Words by Jean Kyler McManus and Grace Noll Crowell,
reimagined by Ray Schwertner, CEO of Garland Power & Light,
Garland, Texas, in honor of David Pruitt's Sixtieth Birthday.

A friend is someone we turn to
When our spirits need a lift.
A friend is someone we treasure
For our friendship is a gift.

A friend is someone who fills our lives
With value, joy, and grace
And makes the whole world we live in
A better and happier place.

I never came to you, my friend,
And went away without
New enrichment of the heart;
More faith and less of doubt.

In great need of coming to you,
I received courage for the days ahead.
As others turned their heads away
You filled me with comfort instead.

How can I find the shining words,
The glowing phrase that tells
What your friendship has meant to me,
And all that your friendship spells?

There is no word, no phrase
For you on whom I so depend.
All I can say to you is this,
God bless you precious friend.

When just being together is more important than what you do, . . . you are with a friend.

—Anonymous

It takes two people to hurt you, your enemy to say something bad about you, and a friend to tell you.

—Mark Twain

Friendship consists in forgetting what one gives and remembering what one receives.

—Alexandre Dumas

Friendship goes beyond our differences and finds a common interest or concern to hold upon.

—Unknown

Never explain—your friends do not need it, and your enemies will not believe it anyway.

—Unknown

A friend is a person with whom I may be sincere. Before him, I may think aloud.

—Ralph Waldo Emerson

There is no friend like an old friend who has shared our morning days, no greeting like his welcome, no homage like his praise.

—Oliver Wendell Holmes

The only rose without thorns is friendship.

—UNKNOWN

Do good to thy friend to keep him, to thy enemy to gain him.

—BENJAMIN FRANKLIN

Two persons cannot long be friends if they cannot forgive each other's little failings.

—JEAN DE LA BRUYERE

The soul needs friendship; the heart needs love.

—ED HABIB

Always maintain your personal relationships on the same plane upon which they were formed. True friends will rejoice in your professional success. Allow them to enjoy them with you. Never reassess their personal and professional lives in terms of your own.

—UNKNOWN

I've been blessed with a lot of wonderful friends. I have far more friends than ability.

—MAC BORING
Odessa Top Hand '97

Friends are lost by calling often and calling seldom.

—SCOTTISH PROVERB

Wounds from a sincere friend are better than many kisses from an enemy.

—Proverbs 27:6

Friendship is a responsibility and a blessing.

—Unknown

My theories on death: Whoever is closest to the person who died always feels guilty for their death.

—David W. Pruitt

The first time you verbalize to someone close that a person dear to you is dying, you break down and cry. After that, you can more easily discuss the death of your loved one with others.

—David W. Pruitt

"Why, Jim," his friend exclaimed, "you were in the wrong."

"Don't you suppose I know that as well as you do? That's just why I needed a friend. If I had been in the right, I would have had plenty of them," Bowie retorted.

—Jim Bowie
Alamo Fame

I choose us.

—David W. Pruitt
(about his wife Pat)

The Pruitt Approach—A Coyote Mentality

Honest criticism is hard to take, particularly from a relative, a friend, an acquaintance, or a stranger.

—Franklin P. Jones

Willingness, honesty, and open mindedness are the essential of recovery. But these are indispensable.

—Alcoholics Anonymous
The Big Book

SPIRITUALITY

Martha Beck

Real religion, by definition, makes things whole again.
It heals.

Six Steps to Making a New Start

Rediscover Your Genius
"I can do all things through Christ which strengthened me."
(Philippians 4:13)

Know what you want.
Find yourself.
Get motivated

Understand Success
"Thou wilt show me the path of life."
(Psalm 16:11)

Do your best.
Create positive images.
Commit yourself to god.

Seek Opportunities
"Seek ye first the kingdom of God and his righteousness; and all these things shall be added unto you."
(Matthew 6:33)

Open your mind.
Develop your personality.
Discipline yourself.

Forget, Forgive, and Live
"Forgetting those things which are behind, and reaching forth unto those things which are before, I press toward the mark. . . ."
(Philippians 3:13–14)

Forget the past.
Forgive yourself and others.

Live today.
Cultivate Optimism
"Give thanks unto the Lord, for he is good."
(Psalm 136:1)

Don't limit yourself.
Get outside yourself.
Think health.

Tap Into the Power of Prayer
"What things so ever ye desire, when ye pray, believe that ye receive them, and ye shall have them."
(Mark 11:24)

Talk, visualize, then listen.
Remove all barriers.
Believe in miracles.

O Lord, thou knowest how busy I must be this day. If I forget thee, do not thou forget me.

—S**IR** J**ACOB** A**STLEY**

God has two dwellings: One in heaven and the other in a meek and thankful heart.

—I**ZAAK** W**ALTON**

Any concern too small to be turned into a prayer is too small to be made into a burden.

—C**ORRIE** T**EN** B**OOM**

I can see how it might be possible for a man to look down upon the earth and be an atheist, but I cannot conceive how he could look up into the heavens and say there is no God.

—Abraham Lincoln

God can only do for you what He can do through you.

—Eric Butterworth

Because of Jesus, I can be happy when I should be unhappy.

—Unknown

Thanksgiving seems to announce the approach to the end of yet another year. It is time for reflecting. It is time to give thanks. So, again this year, I give thanks for my measure of health, for my family, and for friends like you. Giving thanks to our father in heaven, may you always have love to share, health to spare with lots of laughter, and friends that care.

—David W. Bower

Joy is not absence of suffering, but the presence of God. Christianity is the religion that first recognizes the individual and leaves hope for the individual.

—Unknown

Blessed are those who give without remembering and take without forgetting.

—Princess Elizabeth Bibesco

Coincidence is God's way of remaining anonymous.

—**ALBERT EINSTEIN**

Big God, little world.

—**UNKNOWN**

I know God won't give me anything I can't handle. I just wish he didn't trust me so much.

—**MOTHER TERESA**

This is the day the Lord has made; let us rejoice and be glad in it.

—**PSALM 118:24**

The best sermons are lived, not preached.

—**UNKNOWN**

There are glimpses of heaven to us in every act or thought or word that raises us above ourselves.

—**ROBERT QUILLEN**

The fear of the Lord is in the beginning of knowledge, but fools despise wisdom and discipline.

—**PROVERBS 1:7**

How I Would Most Like To Be Remembered

That I was faithful to what God wanted me to do, that I maintained integrity in every area of my life, and that I lived what I preached.

—**Billy Graham**

Each day is a gift from God; that is why it is called: "the present."

—**Unknown**

"Joy"—Jesus, Others & You.

—**Unknown**

God is never far away but is closer when we pray.

—**Unknown**

God gives every bird its food, but he does not throw it into the nest.

—**Josiah Gilbert Holland**

May those who love us, love us, and those that don't love us, May God turn their hearts, and if he doesn't turn their hearts,

May he turn their ankles so we'll know them by their limping.

—**Irish Proverb**

= Spirituality =

Spirit of the living God fall afresh on me.
Spirit of the living God fall afresh on me.
Melt me, mold me, fill me, use me.
Spirit of the living God fall afresh on me.

—**Vickie Winans**

My business is not to remake myself but to make the absolute best of what God made.

—**Robert Browning**

Men do not attract that which they want, but that which they are. Their whims, fancies, and ambitions are thwarted at every step, but their innermost thoughts and desires are fed with their own food, be it foul or clean. The divinity that shapes our ends is in ourselves; it is our very self. Man is manacled only by himself. Thought and action are the jailers of fate—they imprison, being base. They are also the angels of freedom—they liberate, being noble. Not what he wishes and prays for does a man get but what he justly earns. His wishes and prayers are only gratified and answered when they harmonize with his thoughts and actions.

Men are anxious to improve their circumstances, but are unwilling to improve themselves; they therefore remain bound. The man who does not shrink from self-crucifixion can never fail to accomplish the object upon which his heart is set. This is as true of earthly as of heavenly things.

—**James Allen**
As A Man Thinketh

We cannot do great things on this earth, only small things with great love.

—**Mother Teresa**

Life is not what you find, but what you create.

—UNKNOWN

Without problems there could be no miracles.

—UNKNOWN

It takes great power to deliver great power.

—GLENN SCHLOSSBERG

Shalom to you now, shalom, my friends. May God's full mercies bless you my friends. In all your living and through your loving, Christ be your shalom, Christ be your shalom.

—METHODIST HYMN

Man plans and God laughs.

—YIDDISH PROVERB

It only takes a spark to get a fire going, and soon all those around can warm up in its glowing. That's how it is with God's love. Once you've experienced it, you spread his love to everyone; you want to pass it on.

—KURT KAISER

If you live a hundred years and you miss Jesus, you have missed it all.

—RANDY MCLEMORE
3/26/44–5/29/02

When everything is leaving you, leave everything to God.

—UNKNOWN

Spirituality

We have come from somewhere and are going somewhere. The great architect of the universe never built a stairway that leads to nowhere.

—Robert A. Milliken

Who falls for love of God shall rise a star.

—Ben Jonson

I think the first virtue is to restrain the tongue; he approaches nearest to gods who knows how to be silent, even though he is in the right.

—Cato the Elder

The saint never has to appear holy but the hypocrite does.

—Unknown

Service is the rent that we pay for our room on earth.

—Charles Lindley Wood Halifax

At my judgment I should like God to say, I have heard my mouth speak of you.

—Unknown

Do not pray for gold. Pray for good children and happy grandchildren.

—Chinese Proverb

God is with those who persevere.

—The Koran

The best way to know God is to love many things.

—Vincent Van Gogh

I have never yet met a healthy person who worried very much about his health, or a really good person who worried much about his own soul.

—John Haldane

The most acceptable service of God is doing good to men.

—Benjamin Franklin

You have not lived a perfect day even though you have earned your money unless you have done something for someone who will never be able to repay you.

—Ruth Smeltzer

Every charitable act is a stepping stone toward heaven.

—Henry Ward Beecher

Some people carry their religion on their backs like a burden when they should carry it like a song in their hearts.

—Unknown

Then choose for yourself this day whom you will serve . . . but as for me and my house, we will serve the Lord.

—Joshua 24:15

Your arms are too short to box with God.

—Alex Bradford and Micki Grant

God, use me until you use me up.

—Oprah Winfrey

Many people want to serve God but only as an adviser.

—Unknown

You may say in your heart, my power and the strength of my hand made me this wealth. But you shall remember the Lord your God, for it is he who is giving you power to make wealth.

—Deuteronomy 8:17–18

I don't understand prayer any more than I understand electricity. But I do know that man builds a generator that catches out of the air that marvelous power—electricity—and we use that power to do so many things for us. God made electricity, and I believe the God who made a power to light our homes did not forget to make a power to light our lives. The God who made a power to pull our buses did not forget to make a power to help his children along the way of life. Prayer is the means by which we obtain God's power. Lord, teach us to pray.

—Unknown

Don't take yourself too seriously! I take myself with a grain of salt and a belly laugh whenever I can. I remind myself of my fallibility, give God the credit for my successes, accept the blame for my failures, and never do anything that would cause my children to lose confidence in me. And I never forget that I am someday going to be accountable to

God. If I can do all that and make an honest profit too, I have the best of all possible worlds.

—U<small>NKNOWN</small>

Earth has no sorrow that heaven cannot heal.

—U<small>NKNOWN</small>

Praise plus poise plus prayer equals peace.

—U<small>NKNOWN</small>

Why do I have to swear on the Bible in court when the Ten Commandments cannot be displayed outside?

—U<small>NKNOWN</small>

To lay Christ in the bottome, as the only foundation of all sound knowledge and Learning. And seeing the Lord only giveth wisdom.

—A<small>NONYMOUS</small>
New England's First Fruits

In this age, there can be no substitute for Christianity . . . that was the religion of the founders of the republic, and they expected it to remain the religion of their descendants.

—H<small>OUSE</small> J<small>UDICIARY</small> C<small>OMMITTEE</small> R<small>EPORT</small>
March 27, 1854

Christianity is a part of the common law . . . I verily believe Christianity necessary to the support of civil society.

—J<small>OSEPH</small> S<small>TORY</small>
US Supreme Court Justice

Spirituality

Blessed is the nation whose God is the Lord.

—Psalm 33:12a

If my people who are called by my name will humble themselves and pray and seek my face and turn from their wicked ways, then I will hear from heaven and will forgive their sin and heal their land.

—2 Chronicles 7:14

And can the liberties of a nation be thought secure when we have removed their only firm basis, a conviction in the minds of the people that these liberties are of the gift of God?

—Thomas Jefferson

Providence has given to our people the choice of their rulers, and it is the duty, as well as the privilege and interest of our Christian nation, to select and prefer Christians for their rulers.

—John Jay
Coauthor of the *Federalist Papers*
First Chief Justice of the US Supreme Court

When you have kids, life changes; you will find that your happiness is then defined by your least happy child!

—David W. Pruitt

A coward is incapable of exhibiting love; it is the prerogative of the brave.

—Mohandas K. Gandhi

Everyone is the age of their heart.

—**Guatemalan Proverb**

You don't have to have proof to believe the negative.

—**Unknown**

Eavesdroppers never hear anything good on themselves.

—**Unknown**

Unity in light of a lack of uniformity.

—**CFC Quote**

It's best to stop talking once you've said all you know.

—**Unknown**

Some things are just too good or important to not share.

—**Unknown**

INSPIRATION

Unknown

The greatest danger for most of us is not that our aim is too high and we miss it but that it is too low and we reach it.

Grow old along with me! The best is yet to be, the last of life for which the first was made: Our times are in his hand.

—ROBERT BROWNING

Take away my capacity for pain and you rob me of the possibility for joy.

—ROSS W. MARRS

One cannot tell what passes through the heart of a man by the look on his face.

—JAPANESE PROVERB

Love cures people—both the ones who give it and the ones who receive it.

—KARL MENNINGER

Joy seems to me a step beyond happiness. Happiness is the sort of atmosphere you can live in sometimes when you're lucky. Joy is a light that fills you with hope, faith, and love.

—ADELA ROGERS ST. JOHNS

Happiness is of the moment. Joy is remembering the moment.

—PREACHER AT ERIN DRUMMOND'S WEDDING

My riches consist not in the extent of my possessions but in the fewness of my wants.

—JOSEPH BROTHERTON

Inspiration

It is right to be content with what we have never with what we are.

—James Mackintosh

You can measure a man's height, you can measure a man's weight, but you can't measure a man's heart.

—Unknown

History judges you on the decisions you make. It doesn't judge you on what would have happened in the absence of a decision.

—George W. Bush

We like someone because. We love someone although.

—Henri De Montherlant

The real measure of a man's wealth is what he has invested in eternity.

—Anonymous

Have a heart that never hardens, and a temper that never tires, and a touch that never hurts.

—Charles Dickens

He who receives a benefit should never forget it; he who bestows should never remember it.

—Pierre Charron

The Pruitt Approach—A Coyote Mentality

The best way to win a war is not to fight it.

—Carl Icahn

Write it on your heart that every day is the best day in the year.

—Ralph Waldo Emerson

A gentle hand may lead even an elephant by a hair.

—Iranian Proverb

When we are tired, we are attacked by ideas we conquered long ago.

—Friedrich Nietzsche

Things work out best for those who make the best of the way things work out.

—John Wooden

We are shaped and fashioned by what we love.

—Goethe

Remember this: very little is needed to make a happy life.

—Marcus Aurelius

You never really leave a place you love. Part of it you take with you, leaving a part of yourself behind.

—Anonymous

═══ Inspiration ═══

If you are content, you have enough to live comfortably.

—Plautus

A contented person enjoys the scenery on a detour.

—Anonymous

By forgetting ourselves in thinking of the feelings of others, we gain happiness.

—Henry D. Chapin

If there is anything better than being loved, it is loving.

—Unknown

He has the right to criticize who has the heart to help.

—Abraham Lincoln

There is no pillow so soft as a clear conscience.

—French Proverb

Who is the happiest of men? He who values the merits of others and in their pleasure takes joy even as though it were his own.

—Goethe

Be sure you're right then go ahead.

—Davy Crockett

To be satisfied with what one has, that is wealth.

—Mark Twain

Your life is what your thoughts make it.

—Marcus Aurelius

The only way to discover the limits of the possible is to go beyond them to the impossible.

—Arthur C. Clarke

A man who dwells on his past robs his future.

—Unknown

Everybody is worried about life after death. I worry about life before death.

—Unknown

It is not in the pursuit of happiness that we find fulfillment, it is in the happiness of pursuit.

—Denis Waitley

When you are able to applaud yourself, it is much easier to applaud others.

—Denis Waitley

We may not have it all together, but together we have it all.

—Unknown

= Inspiration =

Time is a great story teller.

—Irish Proverb

The beauty of the soul shines out when a man bears with composure one heavy mischance after another, not because he does not feel them, but because he is a man on high and heroic temper.

—Aristotle

You receive honors and glory for what you give not for what you receive.

—Unknown

The quality of life depends on quality of the questions you ask yourself daily.

—Unknown

Our mental framework creates our reality. It is then our response to that reality that dictates the quality of our life.

—Unknown

It is only by doing things that one learns how to do things.

—E. W. Scripps

It is only when you despair of all ordinary means, it is only when you convince it that it must help you or you perish, that the seed to live in you stirs itself to provide a new resource.

—Robert Collier

The Pruitt Approach—A Coyote Mentality

Be there a will and wisdom finds a way.

—GEORGE CRABBE

Once you hear the details of a victory, it's hard to distinguish it from a defeat.

—JEAN-PAUL SARTRE

Always imitate the behavior of the winners when you lose.

—GEORGE MEREDITH

When you win, nothing hurts.

—JOE NAMATH

The best index to a person's character is how he treats people who can't do him any good and how he treats people who can't fight back.

—ABIGAIL VAN BUREN

Tragedy is a tool for the living to gain wisdom not a guide by which to live.

—ROBERT F. KENNEDY

We have the ability to plant seeds with our mouths. Don't plant weak seeds. Use your tongue to help build up another person.

—PAT PRUITT

===== Inspiration =====

Doctors say that cheerful people resist disease better than gloomy people.

—Anonymous

To pursue joy is to lose it. The only way to get it is to follow steadily the path of duty.

—Alexander Maclaren

They are never alone who are accompanied by noble thoughts.

—Sir Phillip Sidney

Love considers the well-being of others as important as that of its own.

—Anonymous

I do not know of any way so sure of making others happy as being so one's self.

—Sir Arthur Helps

All the beautiful sentiments in the world weigh less than a single lovely action.

—James Russell Lowell

Nothing is worth more than this day.

—Goethe

How beautiful a day can be when kindness touches it!

—George Elliston

Giving is the secret of a healthy life, not necessarily money, but whatever a man has of encouragement and sympathy and understanding.

—John D. Rockefeller Jr.

We would never learn to be brave and patient if there were only joy in the world.

—Helen Keller

Those who love deeply never grow old; they may die of old age but they die young.

—Sir Arthur Wing Pinero

Never borrow from the future. If you live in dread of what may happen and it doesn't happen, you have worried in vain. Even if it does happen, you have to worry twice.

—Anonymous

The best cure for worry, depression, melancholy, or brooding is to go deliberately forth and try to lift one's sympathy to the gloom of somebody else.

—Arnold Bennett

The soul, like the body, lives by what it feeds on.

—Josiah Gilbert Holland

Inspiration

Love is the only thing that can be divided without being diminished.

—Anonymous

Cease to inquire what the future has in store and take as a gift whatever the day brings forth.

—Horace

A secret to life: It takes little to make me happy.

—David W. Pruitt

Be civil to all, sociable to many, familiar with few, friend to one, enemy to none.

—Benjamin Franklin

Life can be a fun game.

—Unknown

Speak truth with love.

—Unknown

Teach us to delight in simple things.

—Rudyard Kipling

Nothing is so strong as gentleness, nothing so gentle as real strength.

—St. Francis de Sales

Defeat mutual problems, not each other, to make the outcome a win-win solution.

—UNKNOWN

Anyone who doesn't believe in miracles is not a realist!

—DAVID BEN-GURION

As the heat intensifies, we will forge ahead, knowing that the brittle, seemingly strong become steel just by withstanding the fire!

—PATRICIA R. PRUITT

Gratitude is when memory is stored in the heart and not in the mind.

—LIONEL HAMPTON

The day began with dismal doubt, a stubborn thing put to rout, but all my worries flew away when someone smiled at me today.

—ANONYMOUS

Shared joy is joy doubled. Shared sorrow is sorrow halved.

—SWEDISH PROVERB

Blessed are they who are pleasant to live with.

—ANONYMOUS

Inspiration

I always prefer to believe the best of everybody; it saves so much trouble.

—RUDYARD KIPLING

The object of love is to serve not to win.

—WOODROW WILSON

Unless the heart is full, even a rich man is poor.

—ANONYMOUS

Some people make the world more special just by being in it.

—KELLY ANN ROTHAUS

A smile costs nothing but gives much. It enriches those who receive without making poorer those who give. It takes but a moment, but the memory of it sometimes lasts forever.

—ANONYMOUS

It is better to suffer wrong than to do it and happier to be cheated sometimes than to not trust.

—SAMUEL JOHNSON

Real joy comes not from ease or riches or from the praise of men but from doing something worthwhile.

—WILFRED T. GRENFELL

Rings and jewels are not gifts but apologies for gifts. The only gift is a portion of thyself.

—RALPH WALDO EMERSON

Be happy. It's one way of being wise.

—COLETTE

I find the great thing in this world is not so much where we stand, as in what direction we are moving . . .

—OLIVER WENDELL HOLMES

Doing good is the only certainly happy action of a man's life.

—SIR PHILLIP SIDNEY

He lives long that lives well and time misspent is not lived but lost.

—THOMAS FULLER

The ideals which have always shone before me and filled me with the joy of living are goodness, beauty, and truth.

—ALBERT EINSTEIN

Decide to live joyfully, exultantly, gratefully, openly, and then miracles will begin to happen.

—ROBERT MULLER

Inspiration

Courage means to keep working on a relationship, to continue seeking solutions to difficult problems, and to stay focused during stressful periods.

—Denis Waitley

Though we travel the world over to find the beautiful, we must carry it with us or we find it not.

—Ralph Waldo Emerson

When the student is ready to learn, the teacher will appear.

—Buddhist Proverb

If you know you are in it for the long haul, you can weather the shortcomings.

—Sarah Swindell

The most consummately beautiful thing in the universe is the rightly fashioned life of a good person.

—George Herbert Palmer

One of the sanest, surest, and most generous joys of life comes from being happy over the good fortune of others.

—Unknown

When one helps another, both are strong.

—German Proverb

There is as much greatness of mind in acknowledging a good turn as in doing it.

—Seneca

Joys divided are increased.

—Josiah Gilbert Holland

Forgiveness is the fragrance the violet sheds on the heel that has crushed it.

—Mark Twain

To enjoy the things we ought and to hate the things we ought has the greatest bearing on excellence of the character.

—Aristotle

So many of us define ourselves by what we have, what we wear, what kind of house we live in and what kind of car we drive. If you think of yourself as the woman in the Cartier watch and the Hermes scarf, a house fire will destroy not only your possessions but yourself.

—Linda Henley

Destiny is not a matter of change; it is a matter of choice.

—William Jennings Bryan

Happiness is not a destination. It is a method of life.

—Burton Hillis

Rich is not how much you have or where you are going or even what you are; rich is who you have beside you.

—John F. Kennedy, II

— Inspiration —

It requires more courage to suffer than to die.

—**Napoleon Bonaparte**

Practice random acts of kindness.

—**Unknown**

I can live two months on a good compliment.

—**Mark Twain**

Stand for integrity.

—**Bob Adams**

Purpose—develop your dreams and you create passion, develop the dreams of others and you create heaven.

—**Unknown**

Kindness is the language which the deaf can hear and the blind can see.

—**Unknown**

You'll never get ahead of anyone as long as you try to get even with him.

—**Coach Lou Holts**

A slip of the foot you may soon recover, but a slip of the tongue you may never get over.

—**Benjamin Franklin**

The Pruitt Approach—A Coyote Mentality

I think the older you get the bigger you should be (physically), so people know why they should honor and respect you (i.e., at ninety years old, you should be ten feet tall vs. the opposite).

—David W. Pruitt

Tomorrow is the most important thing in life. Comes into us at midnight very clean. It's perfect when it arrives, and it puts itself in our hands. It hopes we've learnt something from yesterday.

—Inscription on John Wayne's headstone

If you wish to travel far and fast, travel light. Take off all of your envies, jealousies, unforgiveness, selfishness, and fear.

—Cesare Pavese

Twenty years from now you will be more disappointed by the things you didn't do than by the ones you did do. So throw off the bowlines. Sail away from the safe harbor. Catch the trade winds in your sails. Explore, dream, discover.

—Unknown

Live all you can; it's a mistake not to. It doesn't so much matter what you do in particular, so long as you have your life. If you haven't had that, what have you had?

—Henry James

Reading makes a full man; meditation a profound man; discourse a clear man.

—Benjamin Franklin

QUESTION

How shall I lead my life? What is a good life? What is a good life for me?

From *Life's Little Instruction Book*
H. Jackson Brown Jr.

- Be brave. Even if you're not, pretend to be. No one can tell the difference.
- Forget the Jones's.
- Choose your life's mate carefully. From this one decision will come 90 percent of all your happiness or misery.
- Give yourself an hour to cool off before responding to someone who has provoked you. If something really important is involved, give yourself overnight.
- Use credit cards only for convenience, never for credit.
- If in a fight, hit first and hit hard.
- Resist the temptation to put a cute message on your answering machine.
- Admit your mistakes.
- Let people pull in front of you when you're stopped in traffic.
- Don't waste time learning the "tricks of the trade." Instead learn the trade.

The Pruitt Approach—A Coyote Mentality

A pessimist has been defined as a well-informed optimist.

—UNKNOWN

Scientists have determined that smoking is the leading cause of statistics.

—UNKNOWN

An advantage unused is a disadvantage.

—DAVE WEINBAUM

A sense of humor reduces people and problems to their proper proportions.

—UNKNOWN

Make the most of what comes, and the least of what goes.

—SARA TEASDALE

First the work, then the plant, lastly the knife.

—AESCULAPIUS OF THESSALY
Greek God of Healing

If you can't be kind, be vague.

—JUDITH S. MARIN

Glory is fleeting, but obscurity is forever.

—NAPOLEON BONAPARTE

Sincerity and truth are the basis of every virtue.

—CONFUCIUS

True goodness springs from a man's own heart. All men are born good.

—CONFUCIUS

It is only the wisest and the very stupidest who cannot change.

—CONFUCIUS

Conformity is the jailer of freedom and the enemy of growth.

—JOHN F. KENNEDY

Truth is the most valuable thing we have. Let us economize it.

—MARK TWAIN

He who learns but does not think is lost! He who thinks but does not learn is in great danger!

—CONFUCIUS

To see what is right and not to do it is want of courage.

—CONFUCIUS

The superior man is firm in the right way and not merely firm.

—CONFUCIUS

The Pruitt Approach—A Coyote Mentality

Our greatest glory is not in never falling but in rising every time we fall.

—Confucius

Don't make wrong mistakes.

—Unknown

I will not die an unlived life.

—Dawna Markova

I actually feel empowered by rejection because I'm convinced they're wrong. It just makes me want to go out and prove that they're wrong.

—Robert Kosberg

Love, unlike gold, is treasure that gains value by being spent.

—Unknown

One of the most difficult things to give away is kindness—it is usually returned.

—Mark Ortman

Form the habit of making decisions when your spirit is fresh. To let dark moods lead is like choosing cowards to command armies.

—Charles Horton Cooley

= Inspiration =

When bad things happen, it's easy to ask, "Why me?" But when good things happen, we seem to feel like we deserve them on some level. So when good things happen, I try to ask myself, "Why me?" It helps put things in perspective.

—JAMES BLAKE
Pro Tennis Player
(twenty-four-year-old with a broken neck)

Courage is not the absence of despair; it is rather the capacity to move ahead in spite of despair.

—ROLLO MAY

The older you get, the stronger the wind gets—and it's always in your face.

—PABLO PICASSO

With every setback is the opportunity to have a comeback.

—UNKNOWN

Being all you can be is possible for anyone, but . . .

—DAN PENA

A very strong catalyst is to sincerely tell him, "I believe you."

—DAVID W. PRUITT

You'll never stub your toe if you walk backward.

—HARVEY MACKAY

Life is either a daring adventure or nothing at all.

—**Helen Keller**

Speed is useful only if you are running in the right direction.

—**Joel Barker**

Time heals old wounds, but also time wounds old heels.

—**Unknown**

Average is the worst of the best and best of the worst.

—**Unknown**

Morality vs. Reality

—**Glenn Schlossberg**

You've got to do your own growing, no matter how tall your grandfather was.

—**Irish Proverb**

Conventional wisdom is almost always wrong.

—**Unknown**

We can achieve nothing without paying the price.

—**Earl Nightingale**

I'll not listen to reason; reason always means what someone else has to say.

—**Elizabeth Gaskett**

====== Inspiration ======

Always shoot for the moon; even if you don't hit it, you will at least get 80 percent.

—Unknown

I'll speak for the man, or against him, whichever will do him most good.

—Richard M. Nixon

The human brain can be trained if it belongs to a student who wants to learn.

—Isaac Newton

A man convinced against his will is of the same opinion still.

—Dale Carnegie

Nobody holds a good opinion of a man who has a low opinion of himself.

—Anthony Trollope

The breath (breathing technique) controls the mind, as the mind controls the body.

—Roshi Kwong

The future ain't what it used to be.

—Unknown

You don't know what you've got, 'til it's gone!

—Unknown

Sometimes the past is the present.

—Unknown

Thinking is the hardest work there is, which is probably the reason why so few engage in it.

—Henry Ford

A remark generally hurts in proportion to its truth.

—Will Rogers

VISION

Richard R. Hibbard

If you can't see a more profitable way to
do something you're not looking!

The market is almost never where the inventor thinks it will be.

—**Peter Drucker**

If everyone waited to tackle the unknown until they had a clear chart of directions, there would be no inventors, explorers, composers, or authors. Creative thinkers are people who move fearless into the unexplored in uncharted territory and have faith enough in themselves to blaze new trails.

—**Unknown**

Have a five-year plan.

—**Bob Adams**

Structure follows strategy. If you base your strategy on your existing structure, you limit your potential to what you've already done.

—**Unknown**

If your vision is right, you'll win.

—**Unknown**

I skate to where the puck is going to be, not where it has been.

—**Wayne Gretzsky**

Vision

Ideas are nothing without action. Action is nothing without completion and completion is nothing without goals.

—Unknown

Be a clock builder versus just a time teller (visionary) when it comes to building a long-life corporation.

—James C. Collins and Jerry I. Porras

Business deals start and end with people—the interaction of flesh and blood, bone and sinew, heart and mind, emotion and soul.

—Dan Pena

Opportunities don't just happen. Often you must make your opportunities; therefore, make it happen or the opportunity will go to someone who is prepared.

—Unknown

Instead of being prisoners of their past successes, champions of change use past experiences to cover trails leading to new opportunities.

—Unknown

Only those who will risk going too far can possibly find out how far one can go.

—T. S. Eliot

The Pruitt Approach—A Coyote Mentality

When written in Chinese, the word crisis is composed to two characters. One represents danger and the other represents opportunity.

—**John F. Kennedy**

You may be disappointed if you fail, but you are doomed if you don't try.

—**Beverly Sills**

In business, the competition will bite you if you keep running; if you stand still, they will swallow you.

—**Unknown**

Loyalty is for dogs. Trust is for small children. Credibility is what you stand on to build for the future.

—**LCRA Chairman**
July 1996

The best pilot in the world can't make a submarine fly; it's not the employees; it's the business structure that's often the problem.

—**Peter Schutz,**
Chairman, Porsche

One's true worth can often be measured by the things pursued.

—**Anonymous**

Vision

Common sense is the knack of seeing things as they are and doing things as they ought to be done.

—UNKNOWN

Our main business is not to see what lies dimly ahead at a distance but to do what lies clearly at hand. The average person has four good ideas per year to improve his situation, but people normally don't act on their ideas. Give us the idea to use at Cap Rock Energy, and we will screen the ideas and then take action.

—DAVID W. PRUITT

The recipe for well-being requires neither positive nor negative thinking alone, but a mix of ample optimism to provide hope, a dash of pessimism to prevent complacency, and enough realism to discriminate those things we can control from those we cannot.

—DAVID G. MYERS

Every problem contains within itself the seeds of its own solution.

—STANLEY ARNOLD

I've seen an increasing inclination on the part of (CFC & NRECA) the electric cooperative leadership to exclude those who don't fit their model and declare them their adversary in a more rigid way than ever before, and this will lend to their own destruction.

—DAVID W. PRUITT

The Pruitt Approach—A Coyote Mentality

Keep your eyes on the stars and your feet on the ground.

—**Theodore Roosevelt**

To remain independent, we must consolidate. This could be your last chance to stay the same if we acquire your company now.

—**David W. Pruitt**

Building a trust-based corporate culture focused on commitment, contribution, and continuity among employees, customers, and partners (stockholders) is essential.

—**David W. Pruitt**

Market clusters of common interest not on demographics. Go as far as you can see; when you get there, you will be able to see further.

—**Unknown**

Dig your well before you are thirsty. The hardest thing in the world to do is to think a thought through to its end.

—**Unknown**

Never underestimate how wrong you can be. Even the most careful planning can be overtaken by external events and circumstances.

—**Dan Pena**

Nothing . . . will ever be attempted if all possible objections must be first overcome.

—**Samuel Johnson**

Vision

If it's your dream and passion, you will not question stretching way outside your comfort zone. Without going beyond, you'll be where you are—years from now.

—Unknown

Ideas are a dime a dozen. People who put them into action are priceless.

—Unknown

Your biggest strength is your biggest weakness.

—Unknown

Virtual is the opposite of concrete.

—Unknown

There is something that is much more scarce, something finer by far, something rarer than ability. It is the ability to recognize ability.

—Elbert Hubbard

Small deeds done are better than large deeds planned.

—Peter Marshall

The firefly only shines when on the wing; so is it with the mind: when once we rest, we darken.

—Philip James Bailey

Who dares to teach must never cease to learn.

—Richard Henry Dana and John Cotton Dana

The Pruitt Approach—A Coyote Mentality

It does not take much strength to do things, but it requires great strength to decide on what to do.

—Elbert Hubbard

Obstacles are those frightful things you see when you take your eyes off your goal.

—Henry Ford

No one is exempt from talking nonsense; the misfortune is to do it solemnly.

—Unknown

The best time to make friends is before you need 'em.

—Ethel Barrymore

The magic formula in human relations is simple. When you begin to dislike someone, do something nice for him.

—John K. Sherman

The nature of men is always the same; it's their habits that separate them.

—Confucius

The secret to success in conversation is to be able to disagree without being disagreeable.

—Unknown

Common sense is not so common.

—Voltaire

Vision

Habit is a cable. We weave a thread of it every day, and at last we cannot break it.

—Horace Mann

The difficult thing is to avoid evil, not death. Evil, you see, runs after us more swiftly than does death.

—Unknown

No man ever sank under the burden of the day. It is when tomorrow's burden is added to the burden of today that the weight is more than a man can bear.

—George MacDonald

When wings are grown, birds and children fly away.

—Chinese Proverb

The very best medicine that a family can keep in the house is cheerfulness.

—Unknown

People who complain that they have had a lot of hard knocks during their lifetime probably don't realize that some of those knocks might have been opportunity.

—Unknown

The only people with whom you should try to get even are those who have helped you.

—John E. Southard

The true way to mourn the dead is to take care of the living who belong to them.

—Edmund Burke

Before we set our hearts too much upon anything, let us examine how happy those are who already possess it.

—François de La Rochefoucauld

Don't hesitate to go out on a limb sometimes. After all, that is where the fruit is.

—Unknown

Positive anything is better than negative nothing.

—Elbert Hubbard

Honesty is the first chapter in the book of wisdom.

—Thomas Jefferson

Whether circumstances make one bitter or better depends entirely upon the "I."

—Evan Esar

If the only tool you have is a hammer, you tend to see every problem as a nail.

—Abraham Maslow

Live your life so that whenever you lose, you are ahead.

—Will Rogers

Vision

The best way to win a war is don't fight it.

—CARL ICAHN

It's what you learn after you know it all that counts.

—JOHN WOODEN

All boats rise with a rising tide.

—UNKNOWN

We make decisions out of inspiration and desperation, but the older you get the less inspiration works because you don't believe the hype anymore.

—DAN PENA

The best things in life are not things.

—ART BUCHWALD

Nobody ever asks a father how he manages to combine marriage and a career.

—SAM EWING

The best time for you to hold your tongue is the time you feel you must say something or bust.

—JOSH BILLINGS

Treasure the chaos out of which order emerges; cherish the puzzlement leading to the light.

—LUCIA CAPACCHIONE

The Pruitt Approach—A Coyote Mentality

If you are patient in one moment of anger, you will escape a hundred days of sorrow.

—**Chinese Proverb**

Occasionally there can be truth but not fact.

—**Unknown**

Beware of a man who is always looking for zebras instead of horses when hoof noise is heard when only horses are near.

—**Unknown**

When will I know I have enough, and what will I do then?

—**Unknown**

When you starve with the tiger, the tiger starves last.

—**Unknown**

It is good to see in the misfortunes of others what we should avoid.

—**Publilius Syrus**

He who blows into the fire will get sparks in his eyes.

—**German Proverb**

Love is a fire. But whether it is going to warm your hearth or burn down your house, you can never tell.

—**Joan Crawford**

=== Vision ===

Talk to the media, not your lawyers.

—GLENN SCHLOSSBERG

Youth is the time for the adventures of the body but age for the triumphing of the mind.

—LOGAN PERSALL SMITH

A partial truth in the hands of an expert is sometimes worse than an outright lie.

—BLACKIE SHERROD

People tend to stay angry a lot longer than they stay appreciative.

—AL LERNER
Owner, Cleveland Browns

Prosperity is a great teacher; adversity is a great one. Possession pampers the mind; privation trains and strengthens it.

—WILLIAM HAZLITT

As we advance in knowledge, wisdom becomes increasingly necessary.

—BERTRAND RUSSELL

Ignorance is a steep hill with perilous rocks at the bottom.

—RAISULI
The Wind and the Lion (1975 film)

He either fears his fate too much or his deserts are small
Who dares not put it to the touch to win or lose it all?
We are not saved by deeds;
We are saved for deeds.
Work consists of whatever a body is
Obligated to do and play consists of
Whatever a body is not obligated to do.

—MARK TWAIN

Everything that can be invented has been invented.

—UNKNOWN

Advice most needed is least heeded.

—ENGLISH PROVERB

Stumbling over the truth can break your heart.

—UNKNOWN

More of the same usually gives you more of the same.

—UNKNOWN

I would rather be the man who bought the Brooklyn Bridge than the man who sold it.

—WILL ROGERS

Don't set time limits for achieving goals; they should transcend time.

—UNKNOWN

Vision

You always need a reason to overlook the obvious.

—Unknown

Life is what happens while you're making plans.

—Allen Saunders

On Money: "There are two things (I won't do for money). I won't kill for it, and I won't marry for it. Other than that, I'm open to about anything.

— Jack Mingo
Prime Time Proverbs

It is a common experience that a problem difficult at night is resolved in the morning after the committee of sleep has worked on it.

—John Steinbeck

Last week I saw a man who had not made a mistake in 4,000 years. He was a mummy in a British museum.

—H. L. Wayland

It's good to have money and the things that money can buy, but it's good to check once in a while and make sure you haven't lost the things that money can't buy.

—Unknown

I'm looking forward to looking back on all this.

—Sandra Knell

The ability to hear again can be relearned not purchased.

—Thomas Jones

Most court room victories are fashioned from the preponderance of perjury and the side most adept, at their spin in the end, at invention, wins. The thought that throughout history truth has withered and died of loneliness in most courtrooms.

—Unknown

The biggest liar in the world is "they say."

—Douglas Malloch

Sometimes things do not break if there's not already a crack.

—Ann Prough

What the teacher is, is more important than what he teaches.

—Karl Menninger

Retirement needs to become a verb. Aging is a process, and our world of work needs to mirror our new lives. Commercialism needs to embrace the "Third Age."

—Steven Cash Nickerson

GOVERNMENT

RONALD REAGAN

Government's first duty is to protect the people not run their lives.

Washington is believed to have said, "Government is not reason; it is not eloquence. It is force. And force, like fire, is a dangerous servant and a fearful master." Bottom line: do you really want the state taking away your choices and making your decisions?

—STEVE FORBES
Freedom Manifesto

The justice system has absolutely nothing to do with justice.

—UNKNOWN

My reading of history convinces me that most bad government results from too much government.

—THOMAS JEFFERSON

The democracy will cease to exist when you take away from those who are willing to work and give to those who would not.

—THOMAS JEFFERSON

Do you want the bureaucracy that gave you the post office to direct your medical treatment and run critical industries?

—STEVE FORBES
Freedom Manifesto

I predict future happiness for Americans if they can prevent the government from wasting the labors of the people under the pretense of taking care of them.

—THOMAS JEFFERSON

Government

Everyone wants a fair and moral society. But is the best way to get there through a politically driven government bureaucracy or through the democracy of the marketplace, where everyone votes with his or her dollars? More to the point, are government bureaucrats beholden to political interests really the ones to decide what is fair and moral?

—STEVE FORBES
Freedom Manifesto

It is incumbent on every generation to pay its own debts as it goes. A principle which if acted on would save one-half the wars of the world.

—THOMAS JEFFERSON

Statist rhetoric—or some would say the guilt trip—is good at putting people on the defensive. Those who defend free markets and free enterprise solutions are called uncaring and heartless. The decision to support or oppose a new big government regulation is usually portrayed by big government advocates as a choice between selfishness and compassion. *You mean you don't want people to be able to get health care?*

—STEVE FORBES
Freedom Manifesto

Obamacare: the law was to result in 159 new bureaucracies, countless regulations, an array of new taxes, and more than 16,000 IRS agents enforcing the mandatory buying of health insurance.

—STEVE FORBES
Freedom Manifesto

No free man shall ever be debarred the use of arms.

—THOMAS JEFFERSON

The strongest reason for the people to retain the right to keep and bear arms is, as a last resort, to protect themselves against tyranny in government.

—THOMAS JEFFERSON

FDR's Keynesian spending and job creation programs sucked capital out of the economy. FDR's price controls and production quotas also created uncertainty that inhibited businesses from hiring. All this delayed recovery until after World War II.

—STEVE FORBES
Freedom Manifesto

The tree of liberty must be refreshed from time to time with the blood of patriots and tyrants.

—THOMAS JEFFERSON

Wall Street Journal columnist Steve Moore asks, "Is it fair that the richest 10 percent of Americans shoulder a higher share of their country's income-tax burden than do the richest 10 percent in every other industrialized nation, including socialist Sweden? Is it fair that nearly half the population today does not pay federal income taxes? Is it fair for big government to grow so big that the total national debt vastly exceeds the annual income of all of the American people and the profits of American businesses?

—STEVE FORBES
Freedom Manifesto

To compel a man to subsidize with his taxes the propagation of ideas which he disbelieves and abhors is sinful and tyrannical.

—Thomas Jefferson

Overly large and politicized government ends up undermining a moral society instead of empowering people, big government programs, from welfare subsidies to corporate bailouts, promote dependency and undermine personal responsibility, encouraging both people and companies to make bad decisions.

—Steve Forbes
Freedom Manifesto

Democracy extends the sphere of individual freedom; socialism restricts it. Democracy attaches all possible value to each man; socialism makes each man a mere agent, a mere number. Democracy and socialism have nothing in common but one word: equality. But notice the difference: while democracy seeks equality in liberty, socialism seeks equality in restraint and servitude.

—Steve Forbes
Freedom Manifesto

Resisting demands for a government program that will supposedly help others can be difficult. But the heart-tugging rhetoric deflects attention from the fact that the proposed solution is usually more bureaucracy. Liberals advocating "compassion" and "human rights" might think again if they realized that what they're really fighting for is more rules, regulations, and red tape that restrict our freedoms.

Government bureaucracies have a poor record of respecting the rights of individuals. And bureaucracy deals in strictures—more and more rules.

—STEVE FORBES
Freedom Manifesto

Others questioned the morality of Romney's tax returns, which revealed that he paid a 15 percent tax rate because his income came from investments. Sparse attention was paid, by Romney's critics or by the media, to the rationale behind the capital gains rate. Critics make it sound as though the gains are a certainty; however, most new ventures fail. The capital gains rate is low because investors like Romney help society by risking money on other people's ventures that may or may not pan out. Not all of Romney's investments succeeded. Those that did generated thousands of jobs and hundreds of millions of dollars for countless investors and shareholders. But to his loud and vociferous critics, Romney was just "moving money around" and had gotten an unfair tax break.

—STEVE FORBES
Freedom Manifesto

Is it fair for people to get ahead based on political connections instead of the real value they provide to others?

—STEVE FORBES
Freedom Manifesto

There is an implied subtext in the speeches of both men: Barack Obama believes in government solutions because he is ultimately unsure about the American system and thinks less of individuals who, he implies, are mired in "greed" and "conflict." Profoundly optimistic about the capabilities and character of the American people, Ronald Reagan believed the solution lay with the efforts of individuals allowing the American free enterprise system to work. Barack Obama admonishes citizens to put aside "childish things"; Reagan focused on the strengths in the American character: "I believe we, the Americans of today are ready to act worthy of ourselves, ready to do what must be done to ensure happiness and liberty for ourselves, our children and our children's children." That is the reason, he concluded, that things will get better. Two stark and contrasting visions, one based on a profound belief in the capacity of a free people to do great things. The other—a belief in the need for big government to guide us because we are unable to guide ourselves. Optimism versus pessimism, choice versus coercion, redistribution versus wealth creation, mobility versus stagnation. We must now decide. Which vision will guide America and the world?

—STEVE FORBES
Freedom Manifesto

It's not what we have that will make us a great nation; it's the way in which we use it.

—THEODORE ROOSEVELT

Some go through life getting free rides; others pay full fare and something extra to take care of the free riders.

—UNKNOWN

Sensible and responsible women do not want to vote.

—GROVER CLEVELAND, 1905

There is no likelihood man can ever tap the power of the atom.

—Robert A. Milliken,
Nobel Prize Winner in Physics, 1920

Heavier than air flying machines are impossible.

—Lord William Thomson Kelvin, President
the Royal Society, England, 1895

When I feel the heat, I see the light.

—Sen. Everett Dirksen

The screwing you give is not worth the screwing you take.

—Unknown

Freedom is the absence of restraint on our thoughts and actions.

—Unknown

One shining quality lends a luster to another or hides some glaring defect.

—William Hazlitt

The founding fathers in 1776 had only three felonies—treason, tyranny, and murder. Today we have thousands of federal felonies.

—Unknown

= Government =

What we need is protections and laws that take into account the *process* of aging, rather than whether you are aged or not.

—S<small>TEVEN</small> C<small>ASH</small> N<small>ICKERSON</small>

We need a law that, while protecting the aging population, allows us to treat age as a process and to descend employees properly down the ladder they climbed.

—S<small>TEVEN</small> C<small>ASH</small> N<small>ICKERSON</small>

FAILURE

LEBRON JAMES

You have to be able to accept failure to get better.

Failure is what we make of it. Nothing fails like success.

—STEPHEN COVEY

Failure to plan on your part *does not* constitute an emergency on my part.

—UNKNOWN

The difference between a failure and a high-performance individual is how each deals with fear. We are all afraid. A high-performance person uses fear to galvanize actions.

—UNKNOWN

We learn wisdom from failure much more than from success.

—SAMUEL SMILES

Perfection is devastated by failure while excellence learns from failure.

—DENIS WAITLEY

I learned more from what I failed at than when I didn't fail.

—UNKNOWN

Failure is only a temporary change in direction to set you straight for your next success.

—DENIS WAITLEY

The credit belongs to the man who is actually in the arena; whose face is marred by dust and sweat and blood; who strives valiantly; who errs and comes short again and again; who knows the great enthusiasms, the great devotions, and spends himself in a worthy cause; who at the best knows in the end the triumph of high achievement; and who at the worst, if he fails, at least fails while daring greatly.

—THEODORE ROOSEVELT

Failure is success's only launching pad.

—TOM PETERS

The only thing anyone can do by himself is fail.

—WALLY AMOS
Famous Amos Cookies

One who fears failure limits his activities. Failure is only the opportunity to begin again and more intelligently.

—HENRY FORD

He who has never failed somewhere, that man cannot be great.

—HERMAN MELVILLE

The majority of men meet with failure because of their lack of persistence in creating new plans to take the place of those which fail.

—NAPOLEON HILL

More men fail through lack of purpose than lack of talent.

—BILLY SUNDAY

The Pruitt Approach—A Coyote Mentality

Victory has a thousand fathers, but defeat is an orphan.

—**John F. Kennedy**

In the game of life, nothing is less important than the score at half time.

—**Unknown**

If at first you don't succeed, you're running about average.

—**Unknown**

In Alaska, I was on a glacier and they said it was moving. That's about as much progress as our business made last year.

—**David W. Pruitt**

No other success can compensate for failure in the home.

—**James Edward McCulloch**

You don't know what's important 'till you lose it.

—**Unknown**

You can lead a horse to water, but you can't force him to drink.

—**Unknown**

Some people only pick the low-hanging fruit.

—**Unknown**

Failure

Failure has no friends.

—John F. Kennedy

I never made the (football) team. I was not heavy enough to play the line, not fast enough to play halfback, and not smart enough to be a quarterback.

—Richard M. Nixon

No man is as great as he thinks he is.

—Will Rogers

I.R.I.S.: "First they Ignore you, then Ridicule you, then Imitate you, and then Steal your idea."

—Sign on the desk of Jeff Skilling, ENRON CEO

A failure is a man who has blundered and then is not able to cash in on the experience.

—Unknown

There are two tragedies in life. One is not to get your heart's desire. The other is to get it.

—George Bernard Shaw

Lack of something to feel important about is almost the greatest tragedy a man may have.

—Arthur E. Morgan

The tragedy of life is not so much what men suffer, but rather what they miss.

—Thomas Carlyle

Do not attempt to do a thing unless you are sure of yourself; but do not relinquish it simply because someone else is not sure of you.

—Stewart Edward White

Regret is an appalling waste of energy... You can't get it into shape; you can't build on it; it's only good for wallowing in.

—Katherine Mansfield

I prefer freedom with danger to servitude with tranquility.

—Unknown

Too many folks go through life running from something that isn't after them.

—Unknown

The only something you get for nothing is failure.

—Unknown

A person who doubts himself is like a man who would enlist in the ranks of his enemies and bear arms against himself. He makes his failure certain by himself being the first person to be convinced of it.

—Alexandre Dumas

Failure

Be able to say to yourself "I have done what I could."

—UNKNOWN

Many people fail in life, not for lack of ability or brains, or even courage, but simply because they have never organized their energies around a goal.

—ELBERT HUBBARD

Mistakes are painful when they happen, but years later a collection of mistakes is what is called experience.

—DENIS WAITLEY

The shortest emotion in human nature is gratitude.

—JOE JAMAIL

The more you investigate, the less you have to invest.

—UNKNOWN

The greatest of faults is to be conscious of none.

—THOMAS CARLYLE

A prescription without proper diagnosis is malpractice.

—UNKNOWN

Promises should not be lightly given unless we want them to be lightly received.

—DENIS WAITLEY

Fairly well-off is a relative thing.

—GLENN SCHLOSSBERG

Leisure is a beautiful garment, but it will not do for constant wear.

—ANONYMOUS

Unfulfilled expectation is the most severe form of punishment.

—UNKNOWN

Well begun is half done.

—ARISTOTLE

There's no optimist rumors.

—UNKNOWN

Small minds and big mouths have a way of hooking up.

—UNKNOWN

An ignorant fella is hell-bent on proving his limitations.

—UNKNOWN

Half of things our opponents tell about us are not true.

—COUSIN BOYLE ROCHE

They will get as good as they give.

—UNKNOWN

FEAR

Franklin D. Roosevelt

The only thing we have to fear is fear itself.

Fear is false expectation appearing real.

—Unknown

What would you do if you weren't afraid?

—Unknown

When you move beyond your fear, you feel free.

—Spencer Johnson

Your most valuable natural asset is your own gut instinct. Know not to be afraid of it. Your instinct has more power than all of the conventional wisdom in the world.

—Unknown

Fear of failure is caused by lack of self-esteem and confidence. Dealing with fear is the key to super success.

—Unknown

If you do not do what you fear, then that fear controls you.

—Unknown

The policy of being too cautious is the greatest risk of all.

—Jawaharlal Nehru

Don't sacrifice the opportunities of tomorrow to the fears of today.

—Unknown

The hero and the coward both feel the same thing, but the hero uses his fear, projects it onto his opponent, while the coward runs. It's the same thing, fear, but it's what you do with it that matters.

—CONSTANTINE "CUS" D'AMATO

Arrogant people are fearful people. The more arrogant, the more fearful. In truth, arrogant people are fragile.

—DR. THEODORE RUBIN

Let us never negotiate out of fear. But let us never fear to negotiate.

—JOHN F. KENNEDY

Never, ever share doubts with anyone.

—UNKNOWN

Courage is resistance to fear, mastery of fear—not absence of fear.

—MARK TWAIN

Nothing makes us so lonely as our secrets.

—PAUL TOURNIER

CHANGE

Jim Rohn

Your life does not get better by chance;
it gets better by change.

The Pruitt Approach—A Coyote Mentality

A competitive world offers two possibilities. You can lose. Or, if you want to win, you can change.

—Lester C. Thurow

Change is inevitable, so let's decide what we want to change and how and let's effect it. Turn change into our ally and decide the future and make it come true. If you want to change things, first you have to change. Lasting change is possible only when the need for change is both understood and internalized. Change the changeable, accept the unchangeable, and remove yourself from the unacceptable. Do not waste time on things you cannot change. The need to change is a prediction of the future, not a judgment of the past.

—David Saxowsky

Change favors only the prepared mind.

—Louis Pasteur

Everyone thinks of changing the world, but no one thinks of changing himself.

—Leo Tolstoy

Change is inevitable—except from a vending machine.

—Robert C. Gallagher

Folks don't change. They just get more so.

—Unknown

Change

You can change the world if you don't have to have the credit.

—U<small>NKNOWN</small>

Change is occurring all of the time. It is necessary to be sensitive to change to be able to respond to it. We must realize that there is an ongoing need to wake up to changes before it is too late.

—U<small>NKNOWN</small>

There is an interesting phenomenon that happens when you put a frog into a pot of cold water and then gradually turn up the heat. The frog will not jump out. Ultimately the frog will be boiled to death. The frog is extremely capable of jumping out, yet the urgency—or the change in the situation—fails to stir the frog into action.

—U<small>NKNOWN</small>

Change is not without inconvenience.

—R<small>ICHARD</small> H<small>OOKER</small>

The past does not equal the future.

—T<small>ONY</small> R<small>OBBINS</small>

Your greatest idea, born out of revolutionary thinking and passion, will die of indifference, apathy, the satiation of low expectations.

—U<small>NKNOWN</small>

The Pruitt Approach—A Coyote Mentality

Just before we stop doing something, we do it in excess.

—UNKNOWN

Crisis is change trying to take place

—UNKNOWN

The hardest thing to learn in life is which bridge to cross and which to burn.

—DAVID RUSSELL

Education's purpose is to replace an empty mind with an open one.

—MALCOLM FORBES

More people spend more time and energy going around their problems than trying to solve them.

—HENRY FORD

Learning is an active process. We learn by doing. So, if you desire to master the principles you are studying, do something about them. Apply them at every opportunity.

—DALE CARNEGIE

Personally I'm always ready to learn, although I do not always like to be taught.

—WINSTON CHURCHILL

Change

Growth means change and change involves risk, stepping from the known to the unknown.

—George Shinn

What are you going to do about the past? It's over.

—Joe Paterno
Football Coach, Penn State University

Don't reduce your expectation out of life.

—Dan Pena

Cash only prolongs death; it does not prevent it.

—Unknown

Make decisions right, not necessarily the initial right decision.

—Bryan Tracey

Beware of the articulate incompetent.

—Unknown

When a man gets up to speak, people listen then look. When a woman gets up, people look; then, if they like what they see, they listen.

—Pauline Fredrick

BUSINESS

Vince Lombardi

The only place success comes before work
is in the dictionary.

Not the people you fire, but the employees you don't fire are the ones who make your life miserable.

—HARVEY MACKAY

A fine is a tax for doing wrong. A tax is a fine for doing well.

—UNKNOWN

Hire slowly, fire quickly.

—BILL JAMES

The unwritten rules of business do not apply to us.

—DAVID W. PRUITT

Don't bust the trust.

—DAVE RAMSEY

Always, always, always pay employees—and yourself—first through all economic cycles.

—DAVID W. PRUITT

You make your money during bear markets, but you just don't know it at the time.

—SHELBY DAVIS

Own bonds for income and own stocks (mutual funds, etc.) for growth.

—JOE LIBERTY

Don't ever bet a $100 to win $10, always bet $10 to win $100.

—H. L. Hunt

Management performance sins will always be forgiven during periods of rapidly increasing revenues.

—Unknown

You don't have to buy customers; you must know customers.

—Unknown

Don't be reasonable.

—David W. Pruitt

When you get rid of someone, never give them a "hook" with which to get back in. Always make a clean, definable, and irrevocable break.

—Unknown

You cannot make a quantum leap if you don't share the wealth with your dream team and employees, be it cash, equity, options, or performance and loyalty.

—David W. Pruitt

The one important thing I have learned over the years is the difference between taking one's work seriously and taking one's self seriously. The first is imperative and the second is disastrous.

—Margot Fonteyn

Some of us will do our jobs well and some will not, but we will all be judged by only one thing: the results.

—VINCE LOMBARDI

Quality: satisfied customers.

—UNKNOWN

It's better for everyone to have eight employees doing ten employee's work than twelve employees doing ten employee's work.

—DAVID W. PRUITT

Team means Together Everybody Achieves More.

—UNKNOWN

The only asset Cap Rock Energy has that can improve (appreciate) with time is an employee.

—DAVID W. PRUITT

The harder you work, the harder it is to surrender.

—VINCE LOMBARDI

No corporation gets hit by the future between the eyes; they always get it in the temple.

—DICK DAVIS

Some companies are under staffed with the wrong people.

—BILL JAMES

Business

Never make a customer tell you the same thing twice.

—UNKNOWN

Business should not run smoothly while you're making your quantum leap. Chaos is normal. The business on quiet waters is still in the harbor.

—UNKNOWN

You must do your job good before you can live the rest of your life.

—DAVID W. PRUITT

We were sucking blood from our own wrists to survive.

—TOM ASHBROOK

People can stand a lot of what with enough why.

—DAVID W. PRUITT

They say that (movies) (new startup companies) are not made, they are forced into existence.

—TOM ASHBROOK

Outsiders looking in say it's exciting; those of us in it say it's treacherous.

—DAVID W. PRUITT

Prosperity without virtue is emptiness.

—RICK PERRY

The Pruitt Approach—A Coyote Mentality

Although risk takers thrive on risks, they don't take chances.

—ROBERT J. KRIEGEL

Nothing is less productive than to make more efficient what should not be done at all.

—PETER DRUCKER

Business deals are built on trust and style.

—DAVID W. PRUITT

Nothing astonishes men so much as common sense and plain dealing.

—RALPH WALDO EMERSON

Always use the chain of command to issue orders, but if you use the chain of command for information, you're dead.

—ADMIRAL HYMAN RICKOVER

If the truth will kill a deal, you don't have a deal.

—DAVID W. PRUITT

Wealth comes from chaos.

—UNKNOWN

The important task rarely must be done today, or even this week. . . . The urgent task calls for instant action. . . . The momentary appeal of these tasks seems irresistible and important, and they devour our energy. But in the light of time's perspective, their deceptive prominence fades; with a sense of loss we recall the vital task we pushed aside. We realize we've become slaves to the tyranny of the urgent.

—CHARLES HUMMEL

Recruit only those you will send to sell a product to your parents and the salesman states he/she is representing you.

—UNKNOWN

Poise and purpose.

—UNKNOWN

It is important not to mistake the edge of the rut for the horizon.

—ANONYMOUS

In the absence of clearly defined goals, we are forced to concentrate on activity and ultimately become enslaved by it.

—CHUCK COONRADT

Risk takers live—or die—by three cardinal rules: rule one, prepare; rule two, prepare; rule three, prepare.

—ROBERT J. KRIEGEL

It is better to know some of the questions than all of the answers.

—JAMES THURBER

Losers make promises they often break. Winners make commitments they always keep.

—**DENIS WAITLEY**

A laugh is worth a hundred groans in any market.

—**CHARLES LAMB**

I've always paid close attention to the whispers around me.

—**STEVE JOBS**
Founder, Apple Computers

A deal is either hot—or it's not!

—**DAN PENA**

From chaos comes order. In chaos is opportunity.

—**UNKNOWN**

Have people to talk to that don't have their hand in your pocket.

—**NORM GAVIN**

Be ready to club them with your velvet-covered hammer.

—**DAVID W. PRUITT**

It's like trying to buy a church: nobody owns it, everybody owns it—cooperatives.

—**DAVID W. PRUITT**

No shots, no ducks.

—Jeff Skilling
CEO, ENRON

Don't worry about the mule, just load the wagon.

—Sonny Garza

Never make a major decision until you have to. Don't miss something because it is not what you had planned.

—Peter Drucker

You may have to fight a battle more than once to win it.

—Margaret Thatcher

There's a big difference between playing to win and playing not to lose.

—Unknown

Stick to your knitting. To maximize the return on invested capital, deploy your assets, resources, and capabilities in those areas wherein your expertise and experience lie.

—Unknown

During quantum growth, any problem you solve will be replaced immediately by a larger, more complicated problem.

—Unknown

The Pruitt Approach—A Coyote Mentality

A deal has to sound good before it is good.

—DAN PENA

Quantum leap success means fishing with nets, not just with lines.

—DAN PENA

Don't take high-performance advice from your peers, family, or friends unless they are high-performance people themselves.

—UNKNOWN

Nothing you'll ever do in a business is a matter of life and death. In the cosmos of time, any decision you make is a fart in the wind.

—UNKNOWN

Find your passion and wrap your career around it.

—DAN BURNS

If you want to travel above and beyond the herd, don't try to be better. Try to be different. Or better yet, be first!

—UNKNOWN

No matter how tempting, never accept short-term solutions to long-term problems.

—UNKNOWN

Business

A guarantor is a fool with a pen.

—Unknown

Watch your business peaks and your troughs. As long as your lows are higher than before, your quantum leap action plan is working.

—Unknown

When you lose, say little. But when you win, say even less.

—Art Modelle

In business, you won't create wealth unless you are willing to share it.

—David W. Pruitt

A business culture should be one of why not rather than why.

—Gordon McCollum
Virgin Corporation

Redefine your company in terms of what it knows and what it owns rather than what it does.

—Unknown

A business model (plan) is not a budget (pro forma-spreadsheet). It is a story. It's a story about an opportunity and how a committed, passionate person or team is going to create and capture value.

—David W. Pruitt

New projects should be asked: Is it sustainable? Is it innovative? And can we make money?

—UNKNOWN

Success is doing the best you can all the time.

—COACH MIKE KRZYZEWSKI
"Coach K"

Too many rules get in the way of leadership and box you in. I think people sometimes set rules to keep from making decisions.

—COACH MIKE KRZYZEWSKI
"Coach K"

Discipline: It's simply doing what you're supposed to do as well as you can when you're supposed to do it.

—COACH MIKE KRZYZEWSKI
"Coach K"

If you develop your business as a team where everybody in the business feels like it is theirs, you create ownership. If something is yours, you treat it better, protect it, work at it, and love it.

—COACH MIKE KRZYZEWSKI
"Coach K"

Find that special person who is the heart of the team; they can bring out the best in everybody else.

—COACH MIKE KRZYZEWSKI
"Coach K"

Business

What you do now as a leader sets up what you do later—and there's always a later.

—Coach Mike Krzyzewski
"Coach K"

Virtual integration will always be better than vertically integrated systems (only if hard rate of return assets are supporting it).

—Jeff Skilling
ENRON

Keep thy shop and thy shop will keep thee.

—Benjamin Franklin

The use of money is all the advantage there is in having money.

—Benjamin Franklin

Leadership is the art of accomplishing more than the science of management says is possible.

—General Colin Powell

Part 1: Use the formula p=40 to 70, in which p stands for the probability of success and the numbers indicate the percentage of information acquired.

Part 2: Once the information is in the 40 to 70 range, go with your gut.

—General Colin Powell

Never let your ego get so close to your position that when your position goes, your ego goes with it.

—GENERAL COLIN POWELL

Perpetual optimism is a force multiplier.

—GENERAL COLIN POWELL

Great leaders are almost always great simplifiers who can cut through argument, debate, and doubt to offer a solution everybody can understand.

—GENERAL COLIN POWELL

POWELL'S RULES FOR PICKING PEOPLE:

Look for intelligence and judgment and most critically a capacity to anticipate, to see around corners. Also look for loyalty, integrity, a high energy drive, a balanced ego, and the drive to get things done.

—GENERAL COLIN POWELL

ENTREPRENEUR'S CURSE

May you have a lawsuit in which you are right.

—JOSEPH MANCUSO

When the facts are on your side, argue the facts. When the law is on your side, argue the law. When neither is on your side, just argue and talk loud.

—DAVID W. PRUITT

Business

It's a merger of talents, cultures, and assets. We think of it more as a merger than an acquisition.

—David W. Pruitt

That feeling our customers have when the lights come back on quicker than they expected—how to communicate what that feels like.

—David W. Pruitt

I've thought about hiring him back so I could fire him and then maybe kill him!

—David W. Pruitt

He who keeps the books always has money.

—Bob Carter
Panda Energy

Strategies can be roughly right, but execution must be perfect.

—Anne Mulchay
President and CEO, Xerox

Men who talk like big wheels usually are mere spokesmen.

—Unknown

The purpose of management is not to get the most out of men but to get the best out of them.

—Unknown

Success formula: Think up a product that cost a dime, sells for a dollar, and is habit-forming.

—Unknown

Training means learning the rules. Experience means learning the exceptions.

—Unknown

No real English gentleman, in his secret soul, was ever sorry for the death of a political economist.

—Walter Bagehot

If economists could manage to get themselves thought of as humble, competent people, on a level with dentists, that would be splendid!

—John Maynard Keynes

On decimal points: I never could make out what those damned dots meant.

—Lord Randolph Churchill

We are all moved by the visible prospect of lost jobs in the auto industry. We tend to forget the unnamed people who lose jobs or don't get jobs, the businesses that close or the new businesses that don't start, because the bailout displaces productive activities elsewhere.

—Eugene Fama

Business

An economists' definition of hatred is the willingness to pay a price to inflict harm on others.

—EDWARD GLASER

There is more to that than people think.

—RONNIE WAYNE CLINTON

When the infrastructure shifts, everything rumbles.

—STAN DAVIS

Financial profit is a product of our stewardship of asset.

—JOHN MYRNA

Do what you do best and subcontract the rest.

—UNKNOWN

Money follows money.

—UNKNOWN

You got one offer; you got no offer.

—MARK RODRIGUEZ

When short-term rates are higher than long-term interest rates, recession will follow in the next twelve months.

—LEHMAN BROTHERS

Your weakest important skill determines the height to which you can use all your other talents and abilities.

—UNKNOWN

Interest on a debt never sleeps.

—UNKNOWN

Sellin' ain't tellin'!

—BRYAN SINGLETARY

Behind every fortune there is a crime.

—RONNIE WAYNE CLINTON

If a man empties his purse into his head, no man can take it away from him. An investment in knowledge always pays the best interest.

—BENJAMIN FRANKLIN

If you look at a chart comparing longevity and wealth, these factors correlate almost perfectly.

—STEVEN CASH NICKERSON

PERSEVERANCE

STEVE JOBS (1955-2011)

I'm convinced that about half of what separates the successful entrepreneurs from the non-successful ones is pure perseverance.

Great works are performed not by strength but by perseverance.

—SAMUEL JOHNSON

Determination and perseverance move the world; to think that others will do it for you is a sure way to fail.

—MARVA COLLINS

We will either find a way or make one.

—HANNIBAL

The thing to try when all else fails is: again.

—UNKNOWN

Never give in, never, never, never—in nothing great or small, large or petty—never give in except in convictions of honor and good sense.

—TOM BRADLEY

Never, never, never, never give up.

—WINSTON CHURCHILL

Fake it till you make it—you are what you think you are.

—DAVID W. PRUITT

I ain't quittin'.

—UNKNOWN

Perseverance

When things go wrong, as they sometimes will,
When the road you're trudging seems all uphill,
When the funds are low and the debts are high,
And you want to smile, but you have to sigh,
When care is pressing you down a bit,
Rest if you must, but don't you quit.

Life is queer with its twists and turns,
As every one of us sometimes learns,
And many a person turns about
When they might have won had they stuck it out,
Don't give up though the pace seems slow,
You may succeed with another blow.

Often the struggler has given up
When he might have captured the victor's cup;
And he learned too late when the night came down,
How close he was to the golden crown.

Success is failure turned inside out
So stick to the fifth when you're hardest hit,
It's when things seem worst that you mustn't quit.
Quitting is not an option.

—Unknown

Don't wait for mentors to seek you out. Don't ever wait for your phone calls to be returned, your letters to be answered, your faxes to be responded to. Keep going out and asking questions.

—Denis Waitley

Nothing splendid has ever been achieved except by those who dared believe that something inside of them was superior to circumstances.

—**Bruce Barton**

Effort only fully releases its reward after a person refuses to quit.

—**Napoleon Hill**

Either I will find a way or I will make one.

—**Sir Phillip Sidney**

Only those who risk going too far can possibly find out how far one can go.

—**T. S. Eliot**

Nothing in the world can take the place of persistence. Talent will not; nothing is more common than unsuccessful men with talent. Genius will not; unrewarded genius is almost a proverb. Education will not; the world is full of educated derelicts. Persistence and determination alone are omnipotent.

—**Calvin Coolidge**

Reframing obstacles is key to turning problems (obstacles) into opportunities.

—**Unknown**

The impossible—what nobody can do until somebody does.

—**Unknown**

Perseverance

You may have to fight a battle more than once to win it.

—Margaret Thatcher

Big risk, big rewards, and big problems. No guts, no glory.

—Unknown

Every day people are straying away from the church and going back to God. Really.

—Lenny Bruce

If you want to make God laugh, tell him about your plans.

—Woody Allen

It's important to be a go getter. But it's even more important to know what it is you want to go and get.

—Gary Kallback

Every little bit helps. Every little quit hurts.

—Unknown

It's always too soon to quit!

—David W. Pruitt

With every setback comes the opportunity to have a comeback.

—Unknown

Become more disciplined. The pain of discipline hurts less than the pain of regret.

—UNKNOWN

Every worthy dream has a pay price to action. That means you have to give up something to get something. You can't have it all.

—UNKNOWN

Good timber does not grow with ease: The stronger wind, the stronger trees.

—DOUGLAS MALLOCH

When the night is darkest, the stars come out.

—UNKNOWN

Storms make oaks take deeper root.

—GEORGE HERBERT

The brook would lose its song if you removed the rocks.

—ANONYMOUS

Many men can rise to the occasion, but few know when to sit down.

—J. FIELDS

We hadn't learned how to give up!

—DAVID W. PRUITT

Perseverance

Strength does not come from winning. Your struggles develop your strengths. When you go through hardships and decide not to surrender, that is strength.

—**Arnold Schwarzenegger**

It's better to prepare for what your enemy can do not what you think he's gonna do.

—**Carl Von Clausewitz**
On War

Those who would give up essential Liberty, to purchase a little temporary Safety, deserve neither Liberty nor Safety.

—**Benjamin Franklin**

Fortune favors the bold.

—**Latin Proverb**

A winner is just a loser who tried one more time.

—**George Moore**

Our greatest weakness lies in giving up. The most certain way to succeed is always to try just one more time.

—**Thomas A. Edison**

Excellence is not an act, but a habit.

—**Coach Johnny Carter**

In any sport to win, unlike offense, defense never has an off night.

—**Coach Johnny Carter**

The Pruitt Approach—A Coyote Mentality

Sports: you might have a bad game offensively, but you can always have a good game defensively.

—Coach Johnny Carter

Those who live by the sword get shot by those who don't.

—Unknown

Bad news never gets better with time.

—David W. Pruitt

History will be kind to me for I intend to write it.

—Winston Churchill

If you get shot, fall forward?

—General George S. Patton

Like in the military, in the time it takes to question an order, you might be dead.

—Phil Jackson
Coach, LA Lakers

Pain has no memory.

—Pat Pruitt

SUCCESS

ESTEE LAUDER

I never dreamed about success. I worked for it.

Being able to enjoy success is the best reason for achieving it.

—Unknown

Success is not making the right or wrong decisions but attitude and procedure.

—Unknown

Know that in order to succeed, you must risk something.

—David W. Pruitt

Success: Pleasing God with the resources he has given you.

—Unknown

Whatever you are by nature, keep to it; never desert your line of talent. Be what nature intended you for and you will succeed.

—Sydney Smith

I missed more than 9,000 shots in my career. I've lost almost 300 games. Twenty-six times I've been trusted to take the game-winning shot and missed. I've failed over and over and over again in my life. And that is why I succeed.

—Michael Jordan

If one advances confidently in the direction of his dreams, and endeavors to live the life which he had imagined, he will meet with a success unexpected in common hours.

—Henry David Thoreau

Success

Most successful people live in the present.

—**Stephen Covey**

If you can move from success in life to significance, you will leave a legacy.

—**David W. Pruitt**

Try not to become a success, but rather to become a man of value.

—**Albert Einstein**

Realize that you, not others, ultimately control your success.

—**Bob Adams**

Celebrate your achievements.

—**Bob Adams**

Plan for success. With no backup plans, no ripcords, no fail-safe's, or you will fail.

—**Unknown**

Move from success to significance.

—**Glen Schlossberg**

I can give you a six-word formula for success: think things through, then follow through.

—**Eddie Rickenbacker**

Success leaves tracks.

—UNKNOWN

Success leaves seeds.

—UNKNOWN

To succeed in business you must do more than take a step in the right direction. You have to take a quantum leap.

—UNKNOWN

In order to really succeed in business, you must have outside advisors. These must be trusted advisors, professionals at your accounting and law firms with whom you have a very special relationship. These advisors become your moles within their own organizations, more loyal to you than their employer. Motivated, aggressive, ambitious, and bright—but not as bright as they think.

—UNKNOWN

The fulfillment of your dream is directly proportional to your desire to succeed and how much you are willing to sacrifice. If you are not prepared to die, then you are not prepared to live.

—UNKNOWN

To achieve hyper-growth, avert avoidable mistakes and let your successes run their own course. Do more of what you are doing right and less of what you are doing wrong.

—UNKNOWN

Hell can be the video of your life if you had taken the actions to become super successful.

—UNKNOWN

Super success is not for everyone. Period.

—UNKNOWN

He has achieved success who has lived well, laughed often, and loved much.

—BESSIE ANDERSON STANLEY

Our limitations and success will be based, most often, on our own expectations for ourselves. What the mind dwells upon, the body acts upon.

—DENIS WAITLEY

The success of our efforts depends not so much on the efforts themselves, but rather on our motive for doing them.

—DENIS WAITLEY

There are two primary choices in life: to accept conditions as they exist or to accept the responsibility for changing them.

—DENIS WAITLEY

Whenever you see a successful business, someone once made a courageous decision.

—PETER DRUCKER

The two most important requirements for major success are first, being in the right place at the right time and second, doing something about it.

—**Ray Kroc**
McDonalds

The difference between successful and unsuccessful risk taking is to determine what is the life blood of this business and what must we do to make it fly.

—**Unknown**

You can do almost everything wrong in business and still succeed if you serve the customer. You can do just about everything right in business and fail if you do not.

—**David W. Pruitt**

Service is not a competitive edge, it is the competitive edge.

—**David W. Pruitt**

When it comes to service, good enough never is. Competing successfully means constant improvement in a thousand places.

—**Unknown**

Your chances of success in any undertaking can always be measured by your belief in yourself.

—**Robert Collier**

Do you risk enough to succeed?

—**Unknown**

Avoiding risk does not equal increasing your security or success.

—David W. Pruitt

Success is the ability to go from failure to failure without losing your enthusiasm.

—Winston Churchill

Successful people do those things which unsuccessful people think are a waste of time.

—Unknown

Success seems to be largely a matter of hanging on after others have let go.

—William Feather

Those who say it cannot be done should get out of the way of those who are doing it.

—Anonymous

No success is accomplished by a reasonable man.

—Malcolm Forbes

I've never seen a "part-time" super-successful, high-performance person.

—Dan Pena

When you attack, you win; when you surrender you die.

—Unknown

First we will be best, and then we will be first.

—GRANT TINKER
NBC

THE FOUR SUREFIRE RULES FOR SUCCESS:

1. Show up
2. Pay attention
3. Ask questions
4. Don't quit

—ROB GILBERT

The highest reward for man's toil is not what he gets for it but what he becomes by it.

—JOHN RUSKIN

A winner concentrates on that which is goal achieving rather than tension relieving.

—DENIS WAITLEY

He who stops being better stops being good.

—OLIVER CROMWELL

Commitment doesn't guarantee success, but lack of commitment guarantees you'll fall far short of your potential.

—DENIS WAITLEY

You can't win at poker or business with scared money. It gives off a stench that is repugnant to the other side. If you are going to play, leave your money at home and play with "OMPH"—other people's money.

—Unknown

Success is always on the razor's edge of failure.

—Ross Perot

The weak ones eliminate themselves.

—Glenn Schlossberg
July 2000

You don't train race horses to come in second.

—Unknown

It's a real source of pride to be perceived as being financially sound and successful.

—Jerry Jones
Owner, Dallas Cowboys

It's not what you get that makes you successful; it's what you are continuing to do with what you got. Success is to be measured not so much by the position that one has reached in life as by the obstacles that one has overcome while trying to succeed.

—Booker T. Washington
(1856–1915), Educator

Ambition is a good servant but a poor master.

—Unknown

Preparation leads to luck.

—COACH CHUCK KNOLL

WANT TO BE A SUPER ACHIEVER?

If you want to be a super achiever, you might want to work on developing traits that a study by Dr. Seymour Epstein, a psychologist, showed super achievers have and here are some of the most important:

They cope with disapproval well. Super achievers are less sensitive to the disapproval and rejections. Their thinking is action oriented. They think in ways that facilitate effective action and don't spend lots of time worrying.

They don't waste time on things they can't change. They don't let little things bother them, and they don't worry about negative situations they can't affect. They learn from their mistakes.

They're less rigid than others in their thinking. They don't classify people as "for" or "against" them. They don't group people in categories, such as "winners" or "losers." They don't feel they should retaliate when people treat them badly and they favor compromise over rigid decisions.

They plan well. Once priorities are established, they work on them.

—UNKNOWN

FOUR COMPONENTS OF SUCCESS

Hustle leads to confidence that generates consistency which starts building competence. All together this equals success.

—UNKNOWN

Four Fs of Success

Faith, focus, follow through, and fulfillment

—Unknown

The speed of the boss is the speed of the crew.

—David W. Pruitt

One man with courage makes a majority.

—Unknown

Make friends of your creditors, but never make creditors of your friends.

—Henry A. Courtney

The wise man thinks everything he says; the fool says everything he thinks.

—Unknown

To have what we want is riches, but to be able to do without is power.

—George MacDonald

You are only a success at the moment that you do a successful act. Glorification comes from the journey, not the outcome.

—Phil Jackson
Coach, LA Lakers

Facts seldom settle arguments. It is the implications drawn from them that most often win the day.

—Unknown

Failure is only the opportunity to begin again, this time more intelligently.

—Henry Ford

The freedom to fail is vital if you're going to succeed.

—Michael Korda

Anyone who is successful, people would like to take them down based on ignorance.

—Jeff Skilling
ENRON

Excitement is the catalyst of courage, which leads to success.

—David W. Pruitt

Fortunes follow the bold.

—Unknown

I was always smart enough to be naïve enough to not know what I couldn't accomplish.

—Kevin Plank
Founder, Under Armour

The answer often to reaching your goals is to will it to happen.

—David W. Pruitt

Success

Ambition is the path to success. Persistence is the vehicle you arrive in.

—**Bill Bradley**
Former Democratic Senator and
Professional Basketball Player

When you are the first to do something, you get to make up most of the rules.

—**David W. Pruitt**

Every time a man puts a new idea across, he faces a dozen men who thought of it before he did. But they only thought of it.

—**Oren Arnold**

There are no gains without pains.

—**Benjamin Franklin**

One today is worth two tomorrows.

—**Benjamin Franklin**

The eye of a master will do more than both of his hands.

—**Benjamin Franklin**

Success is a lousy teacher. It seduces smart people into thinking they can't lose.

—**Bill Gates**

The Pruitt Approach—A Coyote Mentality

The challenge of overcoming obstacles pushes people to discover new capabilities and come up with innovations.

—STEVE FORBES

The secret of success is learning how to use pain and pleasure instead of having pain and pleasure use you. If you do that, you're in control of your life. If you don't, life controls you.

—TONY ROBBINS

Life is about upgrades.

—UNKNOWN

Legacy of the past can kill you.

—UNKNOWN

They haven't found their place in the future. They want to deny our future for us.

—JERRY GLOVER
May 1993

Quality not quantity.

—UNKNOWN

Never throw mud. You may miss your mark, but you will have dirty hands.

—JOSEPH PARKER

Success

The palest ink is better than the best memory.

—CHINESE PROVERB

Integrated for problem solving: "Time, money, patience, and change expectation."

—ALLAN CUMMINGS

Sit yourself in a think chair, it better not be a toilet.

—NORM GAVIN

Keep yourself in good physical condition.

—BOB ADAMS

Always be open to learning new things.

—BOB ADAMS

Develop a support network.

—BOB ADAMS

War is the remedy our enemies have chosen.

—GENERAL WILLIAM T. SHERMAN

I've paid zero dollars in income tax in one year, and I've paid over a million dollars in income tax in one year, and I prefer paying a million dollars in income tax.

—DAVID W. PRUITT

LEADERSHIP

Charles S. Lauer

Leaders don't force people to follow;
they invite them on a journey.

Brainstorm alternatives to tough decisions.

—BOB ADAMS

Every party to every negotiation has a comfort zone. The effective negotiator is the one who can define the boundaries of the other party's comfort zone, then place the detail inside of the boundary of that zone nearest his own interests.

—UNKNOWN

The business world is divided into people with great ideas and people who take action on those ideas.

—UNKNOWN

The old Kenny Rogers song "The Gambler" has a message for CEOs, "You've got to know when to hold 'em, and known when to fold 'em." As a CEO, you'll get more advice from your staff than you know what to do with. But it is up to you to know when to "hold 'em" and when to "fold 'em." Listen to your staff. Listen to your gut. Make your decision and move on.

—UNKNOWN

Too many companies try to patch when they should amputate. "Let's reorganize and save this mess" is a clarion call to disaster. Cut your losses, kick the cuttings out of your way, and move on.

—UNKNOWN

Making Exceptions

The executive exists to make sensible exceptions to general rules.

—Elting E. Morison

Attitude of a Leader

An army of deer led by a lion is more to be feared than an army of lions led by a deer.

—Phillip II of Macedon

You lead by consent, not by title or rank.

—Unknown

Setting an example is not the main means of influencing others; it is only the means.

—Albert Einstein

The customer's opinion of an employee is what is important in his/her evaluation (appraisal).

—Unknown

The most important day I remember in all my life is the one on which my teacher, Anne Mansfield Sullivan, came to me.

—Helen Keller

There is no "I" in team.

—Unknown

The best measure of character is not the behavior that brings us to a crisis, but the manner in which we face it.

—UNKNOWN

To be a leader, first learn to manage yourself; use discipline and creativity to really get the job done.

—ZIG ZIGLAR

You become a champion by fighting one more round.

—JAMES J. CORBETT

Anyone who angers you conquers you.

—CONFUCIUS

The strength of a team comes from utilizing the uniqueness of individuals not necessarily building a consensus. The leader then must involve the team member in the decision reaching process in such a way that the individual derives value from the team not compromises that which weakens the course of action the leader selects.

—UNKNOWN

When performance is measured, performance improves. When performance is measured and reported back, the rate of improvement accelerates.

—THOMAS MONSON

Build consensus as to leadership values and philosophy not necessarily on decision-making before action is taken.

—DAVID W. PRUITT

Leadership

We usually can't lead without learning how to follow.

—Unknown

Make up your mind to act decidedly and take the consequences. No good is ever done in this world by hesitation.

—Thomas Henry Huxley

In a negotiation, he who cares less wins.

—Anonymous

Management: getting things (tasks) done that we can't do alone.

—Peter Schutz
Chairman, Porsche

The difference in know-how and wisdom is in the doing.

—Unknown

I would rather err on the side of over communication than on under communicating.

—David W. Pruitt

One cannot take responsibility without information, but with information, one cannot help from taking responsibility.

—Unknown

Consensus develops a common denominator so low no one cares what is done; thus, collaboration without consensus is the sole of a competitive advantage in business.

—Unknown

I may lose a battle but I will never lose minutes.

—**Napoleon Bonaparte**

Logic is a battle winner and war looser in making a deal.

—**Unknown**

Consensus seeking is a time wasting, leveling influence that impedes distinctive performance.

—**Unknown**

The secret to managing is to keep the people who hate you away from the guys who are undecided.

—**Casey Stengal**

Each of us is responsible for satisfying the customer.

—**Unknown**

An antidote for conservatism—you turn conservative in management style when you realize you have something to lose.

—**Steve Jobs**
Founder, Apple Computers

Rubicon, the red river Caesar crossed when he left a smaller life for the biggest challenge of all. Rubicon is the symbol of a person's commitment to a big idea.

—**Harriet Rubin**

By the work, one knows the workman.

—**Jean De La Fontaine**

Leadership

Happy is the man who can keep a quiet heart in the chaos and tumult of this modern world.

—Patience Strong

The blossom cannot tell what becomes of its odor, and no man can tell what becomes of this influence.

—Henry Ward Beecher

Character is what we are in the dark.

—Dwight L. Moody

I hate to see things done by halves. If it be right, do it boldly. If it be wrong, leave it undone.

—Bernard Gilpin

To leave a legacy: Cap Rock Energy, as the first electric company to go public in sixty years, we must archive and honor everyone who had any part, for example, contract employees, directors and part-time employees, etc., with a plaque, a monument, or maybe a time capsule.

—David W. Pruitt

Anger is one letter short of danger.

—Anonymous

Nothing gives one person so much of an advantage over another than to stay cool and unruffled in a time of crisis.

—Thomas Jefferson

The Pruitt Approach—A Coyote Mentality

You are always accountable to someone.

—Unknown

Who dares to teach must never cease to learn.

—Richard Henry Dana and John Cotton Dana

Manage the downside; the upside will take care of itself.

—Unknown

What I do best is share my enthusiasm.

—Bill Gates

The six steps to becoming a better listener—form a ladder:

Look at the person speaking to you.
Ask questions.
Don't interrupt.
Don't change the subject.
Empathize.
Respond verbally and nonverbally.

—Unknown

Hire attitude and develop skill.

—David W. Pruitt

American's future will be no greater than the one we prepare our children to build. We must not handicap them with obsolete tools.

—Frank Shrontz
Chairman and CEO, The Boeing Company

Leadership

Expect the best, plan for the worst, and prepare to be surprised.

—Denis Waitley

We judge ourselves by what we think we can do. Others judge us by what we have already done.

—Unknown

Nearly every great discovery in science has come as the result of providing a new question rather than a new answer.

—Paul A. Meglitsch

Be sure you're right then go ahead.

—Davy Crockett

Setting an example is not the main means of influencing others; it is the only means.

—Albert Einstein

A statement to make if you lose: what it is, is what it is.

—David W. Pruitt

Almost anyone can stand adversity. To test a person's character, give him or her "power."

—Abraham Lincoln

Next in importance to having good aim is recognizing when to pull the trigger.

—Unknown

The Pruitt Approach—A Coyote Mentality

Time is important, but we must be guided by the compass and not the clock.

—**Bob Phillips**
NRTC

I ask you to judge me by the enemies I have made.

—**Franklin D. Roosevelt**

I'm careful about what I say, but not my words.

—**David W. Pruitt**

MOTIVATION

Bruce Lee

If you spend too much time thinking about a thing,
you'll never get it done.

I think there are several things that hold people back. One is waiting for permission or approval to take a risk. The second thing is that people don't take the first step because they don't have a clear path to achieving their goal. And because they can't see a clear path, they never start doing anything. All you have to do is figure out the two or three things that you need to pursue to get roughly in the right direction, pay attention to what's happening, and react to it one way or the other. You'll succeed at some things you failed at. It is a process. The majority of successful people have had failure and happy accidents, and the way they had them was by getting out of there.

Now I know the single biggest difference between a super high performance person isn't brains or education—though these certainly can make it easier to succeed. It's the resolute, undying belief in what you're doing. The constant perseverance that it will get done—no matter what. Many goals are virtually impossible unless your endeavor is wrapped around your dream and your passion for it.

—**Dan Pena**

Adversity is life's greatest teacher.

—**Unknown**

Remind yourself that every day is a new opportunity.

—**Unknown**

Start by doing what's necessary then do what's possible—and suddenly you are doing the impossible.

—**St. Francis of Assisi**

Motivation

Be your best, regardless of circumstances.

—**Jason Garrett**
Head Coach, Dallas Cowboys

You will be motivated by inspiration or desperation. It's your choice.

—**Unknown**

What you see is what you get, and who you feel like is who you really are. It is not what you are that holds you back; it is what you think you are not.

—**Unknown**

Your time is limited, so do not waste it living someone else's life. Do not be trapped by dogma—which is living with the results of other people's thinking. Do not let the noise of other's opinions drown out your own inner voice. Most important, have the courage to follow your heart and intuition. They somehow already know what you truly want to become. Everything else is secondary. . . . Stay Hungry. Stay Foolish.

—**Steve Jobs**
Founder, Apple Computers

You say this too will pass—which we assume things will be better than now—but times could get worse rather than better, so prepare for both.

—**David W. Pruitt**

Patience is the companion of wisdom.

—**St. Augustine**

The Pruitt Approach—A Coyote Mentality

I cannot pick my mother or father, but I can pick my enemies.

—DAVID W. PRUITT

Discipline: Do what has to be done, when it has to be done, the best it can be done every time.

—BARRY SWITZER

Dream big. Think big. Be big!

—UNKNOWN

Dream big—and dare to fail!

—NORMAN VAUGHAN

Seek to make yourself likeable by your love and genuine concern for others.

—UNKNOWN

He has a right to criticize, who has a heart to help.

—ABRAHAM LINCOLN

Mother love is the fuel that enables a normal human being to do the impossible.

—MARION C. GARRETTY

Never, ever second-guess yourself.

—UNKNOWN

Motivation

The achievement of your goal is assured the moment you commit yourself to it.

—Mack R. Douglas

You have to know you can win. You have to think you can win. You have to feel you can win.

—Sugar Ray Leonard

Mind is all that counts. You can be whatever you make up your mind to be.

—Robert Collier

You win some, you lose some, and some get rained out, but you gotta suit up for them all.

—J. Askenberg

The will to win is important, but the will to prepare is vital.

—Joe Paterno

If you can't win, make the fellow ahead of you break the record.

—Anonymous

The only lack or limitation is in your own mind.

—N. H. Moos

Fall seven times, stand up eight.

—Japanese Proverb

The Pruitt Approach—A Coyote Mentality

There is no such thing as no chance.

—Henry Ford

To finish first you must first finish.

—Rick Mears

The greatest mistake a man can make is to be afraid of making one.

—Elbert Hubbard

Toast:
May you live as long as you want, and never want as long as you live.

—Unknown

Love is the only thing we can carry with us when we go, and it makes the end so easy.

—Louisa May Alcott

Discipline yourself so no one else has to.

—Unknown

The thing that contributes to anyone reaching the goal he wants is simply wanting that goal badly enough.

—Charles E. Wilson

Victory—a matter of staying power.

—Elbert Hubbard

Motivation

At any one moment, we have more possibilities than we have ability to act upon.

—Unknown

Home is where one starts from.

—T. S. Eliot

One thing my daddy didn't teach me was how to give up.

—Herman Cain

When you get involved, you feel the sense of hope and accomplishment that comes from knowing you are working to make things better.

—Pauline Kezer

Keep away from people who try to belittle your ambitions. Small people always do that, but the really great make you feel that you too can become great.

—Mark Twain

Life is not about how fast you run or how high you climb but how well you bounce.

—Unknown

Don't worry about opposition. Remember a kite rises against the wind not with the wind.

—Hamilton Wright Mabie

Everything comes to him who hustles while he waits.

—**Thomas A. Edison**

Anything worth doing is worth doing poorly until you learn to do it well.

—**Steve Brown**

Perfect practice makes perfect.

—**Unknown**

Prepare to win.

—**Unknown**

Obstacles are only opportunities in work clothes.

—**David W. Pruitt**

Experience is not what happens to you; it is what you do with what happens to you.

—**Thomas Huckley**

Praise progress.

—**Unknown**

Happiness is an inside job.

—**Unknown**

Jobs do not have futures, people do.

—**Unknown**

Motivation

Little minds are tamed and subdued by misfortunes; great minds rise above them.

—WASHINGTON IRVING

Start interpreting uncertainty as opportunity.

—UNKNOWN

Appreciation is like salt—a little goes a long way to bring out the best in us.

—ANONYMOUS

Keep your face to the sunshine and you cannot see the shadows.

—HELEN KELLER

Nothing is impossible to a willing heart.

—THOMAS HEYWOOD

The greater the obstacle, the more glory in overcoming it.

—MOLIERE

Seeds of discouragement will not grow in the thankful heart.

—ANONYMOUS

What do we live for, if it is not to make life less difficult to each other.

—GEORGE ELIOT

The Pruitt Approach—A Coyote Mentality

The best thing about the future is that it comes only one day at a time.

—ABRAHAM LINCOLN

If you have accomplished all that you planned for your life, you have not planned enough.

—ANONYMOUS

The best plan in the world carried out tomorrow will never be as good as almost any plan carried out today.

—GENERAL GEORGE S. PATTON

The person who will risk nothing does nothing, has nothing, is nothing. Only a person who risks becomes truly free.

—UNKNOWN

Tough times don't last. Tough people do.

—ROBERT SCHULLER

The thing always happens that you believe in, and the belief in a thing always makes it happen.

—FRANK LLOYD WRIGHT

The things you do when you don't have to will always determine what you are when it is too late to do anything about it.

—UNKNOWN

Losers take chances; winners make choices.

—UNKNOWN

Motivation

Act as if it is impossible to fail and it will be.

—UNKNOWN

You miss 100 percent of the shots you never take.

—WAYNE GRETZKY

If you do everything, you will win.

—LYNDON B. JOHNSON

You can't depend on your judgment if your imagination is out of focus.

—MARK TWAIN

Business opportunities abound, but formidable barriers exist. And the biggest barrier is psychological. It is you.

—UNKNOWN

Absence of evidence is not evidence of absence. Just because something has never been done does not mean it cannot be done. The fact that you have never seen or heard something is not proof that it does not exist.

—UNKNOWN

The best way to predict the future is to create it yourself.

—UNKNOWN

It costs nothing to aim high—but if you aim at nothing, you'll hit anything.

—UNKNOWN

Some people believe that holding on and hanging in there are signs of great strength. However, there are times when it takes much more strength to know when to let go—and then do it.

—Ann Landers

"Thinking it over" is for people who can't take action.

—Unknown

Live your life on purpose!

—Unknown

Give yourself permission to make mistakes. It's called learning.

—Unknown

I have no more mountains left to climb—but me. The positive thinker does not refuse to think about the negative but refuses to dwell on it.

—John Arend

You must decide not to be a victim and be accountable for all your actions in life.

—Unknown

Don't fall in love with the future, work for today.

—Glenn Schlossberg

Today is the tomorrow that you feared yesterday.

—Unknown

Motivation

In the middle of every difficulty lies opportunity.

—ALBERT EINSTEIN

Seek opportunity you'll find security; seek security you will find neither security nor opportunity.

—UNKNOWN

Think it, do it, fix it.

—BILL GATES

Do it, fix it, try it.

—BILL GATES

As long as you're going to think anyway, you might as well think big!

—DONALD TRUMP

Attitude determines altitude.

—DAVID W. PRUITT

You feel pressure or you apply it!

—DAVID W. PRUITT

Do what you love and you'll never have to work.

—UNKNOWN

It ain't over 'till it's over.

—YOGI BERRA

The Pruitt Approach—A Coyote Mentality

A man pretty much always refuses another man's first offer no matter what it is.

—MARK TWAIN

Use what talents you possess: The woods would be very silent if no birds sang except those that sang best.

—UNKNOWN

Six Ways to Make People Like You:

1. Become genuinely interested in other people.
2. Smile.
3. Remember that a man's name is to him the sweetest and most important sound in any language.
4. Be a good listener; encourage others to talk of themselves.
5. Talk in terms of the other man's interests.
6. Make the other person feel important and do it sincerely.

—DALE CARNEGIE

The supreme happiness of life is the conviction of being loved for yourself, or more correctly, being loved in spite of yourself.

—UNKNOWN

To bring up a child in the way he should go, travel that way yourself.

—UNKNOWN

Motivation

The world usually pushes a man in the direction he makes up his mind to go. If he strives to go up, they will push him up; if he lets himself go down, there will be plenty of people on hand to let him slide.

—UNKNOWN

The most difficult part of getting to the top of the ladder is getting through the crowd at the bottom.

—UNKNOWN

Anyone who stops learning is old whether at twenty or eighty.

—HENRY FORD

You have to be in the right place at the right time, but when it comes, you better have something on the ball.

—GROUCHO MARX

Don't belittle yourself. Be BIG yourself.

—CORITA KENT

Don't be first; be the first to be second.

—DAVID W. PRUITT

Remember, there are two benefits of failure: First, if you do fail, you learn what doesn't work. And second, the failure gives you an opportunity to try a new approach.

—ROGER VON OECH

If you don't have time to do it right, when will you have time to do it over?

—JOHN WOODEN

It's hard to detect good luck—it looks so much like something you've earned.

—FRED A. CLARK

If you only knock long enough and loud enough at the gate, you are sure to wake up somebody.

—HENRY WADSWORTH LONGFELLOW

Acceptance of what has happened is the first step to overcoming the consequences of any misfortune.

—WILLIAM JAMES

It's not whether you get knocked down. It's whether you get up again.

—VINCE LOMBARDI

Never give up then, for that is just the place and time that the tide will turn.

—HARRIET BEECHER STOWE

Those who have kokorozashi never give up. Those who never give up hold on to hope. Those who hold on to hope have dreams. Those who have dreams never lose sight of their objectives. Those who never lose sight of their objectives recognize the facts of life. Those who recognize the

Motivation

facts of life are never self-satisfied. Those who are never self-satisfied make every creative endeavor. Those who make every creative endeavor show originality. Those who show originality never cease to grow. Those who never cease to grow set the objectives of higher value. Those who set the objectives of higher value have kokorozashi. Those who have kokorozashi never give up.

—Sakan Yanagidaira
CEO, Super Pac

Never believe anything until it has been officially denied.

—Unknown

Your integrity will affect your destiny. Don't leave home without it.

—Clarence E. Hodges

If you are going through hell, keep going.

—Winston Churchill

The road through life is long and rocky—take plenty of beer.

—Unknown

Worry is a misuse of the imagination.

—Dan Zadra

People who mind don't matter; people who matter don't mind.

—Dr. Seuss

The Pruitt Approach—A Coyote Mentality

It's hard to play good, but you can always play hard.

—Unknown

Don't cry because it's over. Smile because it happened.

—Dr. Seuss

The measure of a man's real character is what he would do if he knew he would never be found out.

—Macaulay

Do you think and or say: what do we get to do today or what do we have to do today?

—Deion Sanders
Hall of Fame, NFL Player

If you don't finish, it's like you didn't start.

—David W. Pruitt

Sometimes to make things happen you have to manufacture urgency.

—David W. Pruitt

Faith can move mountains, but don't be surprised if God hands you a shovel.

—Unknown

Go confidently in the direction of your dreams.

—Unknown

══ Motivation ══

The Constitution only guarantees the American people the right to pursue happiness. You have to catch it yourself.

—Benjamin Franklin

QTL—Quality Time Left.

—Jimmy Johnson
Retired Coach, Dallas Cowboys

The choices we make define character.

—Unknown

Taking care of business regardless of what life gives you.

—Sandra Bullock

Never let the fear of striking out keep you from playing the game.

—Babe Ruth

It cannot be done because the law says you cannot. So change the law.

—Jack D. Ladd

Birthday Toast

May the best of your past be the worst of your future.

—Ron Reuven

None are so old as those who have outlived enthusiasm.

—Henry David Thoreau

The Pruitt Approach—A Coyote Mentality

Everything counts.

—Unknown

Deserve victory.

—Winston Churchill

Go hard or go home.

—Unknown

Pay price to action.

—Unknown

The only easy day was yesterday.

—Unknown

It's not whether you win or lose but if you win.

—Tony Robbins

No one becomes a champion without help.

—Johnny Miller

Shrug off your setbacks.

—Bob Adams

HUMOR

Robert Frost

If we couldn't laugh, we would all go insane.

The Pruitt Approach—A Coyote Mentality

It's not history repeating itself but foolish men repeating history.

—**Bryant Gumble**

There is an old saying: good, cheap, or fast—pick two. You can't have all three.

—**Unknown**

If you think you are in control, you are probably not driving fast enough.

—**Unknown**

Isn't it nice that wrinkles don't hurt?

—**Unknown**

Insanity is hereditary—you get it from your children.

—**Sam Levenson**

It's not whether you win or lose. It's whether I win or lose.

—**Anonymous**

I wish I could play my normal game. Just once.

—**Anonymous**

He who has the fastest golf cart never has a bad lie.

—**Mickey Mantle**

Whenever you want to marry someone, go have lunch with his ex-wife.

—SHELLY WINTERS

You know you're getting old when you fall down and wonder what else you can do while you are down there.

—UNKNOWN

What does a clock do when it's hungry? It goes back four seconds.

—UNKNOWN

I wondered why the baseball was getting bigger. Then it hit me!

—UNKNOWN

Broken pencils are pointless.

—UNKNOWN

Bureaucracy is a giant mechanism operated by pygmies.

—HONORE BALZAC

One of life's most sublime experiences is to be shot at and missed.

—WINSTON CHURCHILL

Planning: Nothing ever comes out like it's supposed to and this didn't either.

—HERB BLANKSHIP
VP, Parking Drilling Co.

The Pruitt Approach—A Coyote Mentality

Too soon old, too late smart.

—Unknown

Groan and forget it.

—Jessamyn West

Happy wife, happy life.

—Jeff Allen

The computer is a moron.

—Peter Drucker

If you can read this, thank a teacher, and since it's in English, thank a soldier.

—Unknown

Before I got married, I had six theories about bringing up children; now I have six children and no theories.

—John Wilnot

If you can't whip them, call mother.

—Unknown

You can't teach a pig to dance.

—Unknown

If you can't stand the heat, use a microwave.

—Unknown

Humor

If you have to swallow a frog, you don't want to look at him long.

—Zig Ziglar

Life is about upgrades.

—Steven Cash Nickerson

Fatigue makes cowards of us all.

—Jimmy Johnson
Former Head Coach, Dallas Cowboys

Whoever called it necking was a poor judge of anatomy.

—Groucho Marx

If you don't know where you are going, you might end up somewhere else.

—Yogi Berra

Why is it when people say "That's a good question," they never have a good answer?

—Walter J. Kennevan

Whoever said, "It's not whether you win or lose that counts," probably lost.

—Martina Navratilova

Governing Italy is very difficult and unnecessary.

—Peter Schutz
Chairman, Porsche

Even if you are on the right track, you can get run over if you are standing still.

—**Will Rogers**

The future ain't what it used to be.

—**Yogi Berra**

Laughter is the shortest distance between two people.

—**Victor Borge**

Depend on the rabbit foot if you will, but remember it didn't work for the rabbit.

—**R. E. Shay**

Load the canon and maybe fire the BB gun.

—**David W. Pruitt**

Don't name a pig you plan to eat.

—**Unknown**

If at first you don't succeed, try raising rabbits.

—**Unknown**

You can't blame a worm for not wanting to go fishing.

—**Unknown**

Better to have loved and lost than to marry a dairy farmer.

—**Unknown**

Humor

The trouble with a milk cow is she won't stay milked.

—UNKNOWN

If it ain't broke, chances are it will be.

—UNKNOWN

It's downright amazing to argue with a fella who knows what he's talking about.

—UNKNOWN

The first thing a kid learns when he gets a drum for Christmas is that he'll never get another one.

—MARIANNA NUNES

Keep skunks and bankers at a distance.

—UNKNOWN

The most powerful thing man ever invented is compounded interest.

—ALBERT EINSTEIN

Who the hell wants to hear actors talk?

—HARRY M. WARNER
Chairman, Warner Bros. Studios 1927

Babe Ruth made a big mistake when he gave up pitching.

—TRIS SPEAKER, 1921

Laughter covers up pain.

—MARIANNA NUNES

Car sickness is the feeling you get every month when the payment is due.

—MARIANNA NUNES

To have fun or humor you must be willing to be embarrassed.

—MARIANNA NUNES

A smile is a curve that sets everything straight.

—MARIANNA NUNES

Financial success will help you find some mighty interesting relatives.

—MARIANNA NUNES

Humor is laughing at what you haven't got when you ought to have it.

—MARIANNA NUNES

Be outrageous—it's the only place that is not crowded.

—MARIANNA NUNES

Spill the pail of milk but don't lose the cow.

—UNKNOWN

Humor

If life gives you lemons, make lemonade.

—Unknown

I believe there is a pony in that room.

—David W. Pruitt

If you're kidding, see if I'm laughing.

—Unknown

Behind every cloud is another cloud.

—Judy Garland

We can't all be heroes because someone has to sit on the curb and clap as they go by.

—Will Rogers

Show me a man who is a good loser, and I'll show you a man who is playing golf with his boss.

—Jim Murray

I have found the best way to give advice to your children is to find out what they want and advise them to do it.

—Harry S. Truman

A family is a unit composed not only of children, but of men, women, an occasional animal, and the common cold.

—Ogden Nash

The Pruitt Approach—A Coyote Mentality

I can remember when the air was clean and sex was dirty.

—**George Burns**

Before you try to keep up with the Joneses, be sure they're not trying to keep up with you.

Erma Bombeck

If you're playing a poker game and you look around the table and can't tell who the sucker is, it's you.

—**Paul Newman**

Men always want to be a woman's first love. Women like to be a man's last romance.

—**Oscar Wilde**

Why do they call it rush hour when nothing moves?

—**Robin Williams**

The secret to staying young is to live honestly, eat slowly, and lie about your age.

—**Lucille Ball**

All men make mistakes, but married men find out about them sooner.

—**Red Skelton**

People will generally accept fact as truth only if the facts agree with what they already believe.

—**Andy Rooney**

Humor

Remember if people talk behind your back, it only means you're two steps ahead.

—Fannie Flagg

When you're born, you get a ticket to the freak show. When you're born in America, you get a front row seat.

—George Carlin

A journey is like marriage. The certain way to be wrong is to think you control it.

—John Steinbeck

There are two great rules in life, one general and the other particular. The first is that everyone can, in the end, get what he wants if he only tries. This is the general rule. The particular rule is that every individual is more or less an exception to the general rule.

—Samuel Butler

When life gets dark, turn to a woman.

—Unknown

Economists have correctly predicted nine of the last five recessions.

—Anonymous

Remember the tea kettle. It is always up to its neck in hot water, yet it still sings!

—Anonymous

There is no danger of developing eyestrain from looking on the bright side of things.

—ANONYMOUS

What a wonderful life I've had! I only wish I'd realized it sooner.

—COLETTE

When you deal with the opinionated or egotistical, always give credit where it is not due.

—UNKNOWN

Creativity is great. Plagiarism is quicker.

—UNKNOWN

The trouble with being in the rat race is that even if you win, you're still a rat.

—LILY TOMLIN

It isn't the mountain ahead that wears you out; it's the grain of sand in your shoe.

—UNKNOWN

Every boxer has a plan to win—until he gets hit!

—UNKNOWN

Whoever said money can't buy happiness doesn't know where to shop.

—A "LINDA PENAISM"

Humor

Even if you're on the right track, you'll get run over if you just sit there.

—Written on the board just inside the door of the New York Giants football locker room

When a person with experience meets a person with money, the person with the experience will get the money. And the person with the money will get some experience.

—Harvey Mackay

When money talks, few are deaf.

—Earl Derr Biggers

Never murder a man who's committing suicide.

—Unknown

Wall Street buys the future, not yesterday's balance sheets.

—Unknown

It takes one woman twenty years to make a man of her son and another woman twenty minutes to make a fool of him.

—Helen Rowland

Insanity is doing the same thing over and over expecting different results.

—Unknown

If you find yourself in a hole, maybe it's time to stop digging.

—Joseph Mancuso

The Pruitt Approach—A Coyote Mentality

The road to success is always under construction.

—UNKNOWN

Hunger makes beasts of men and demons of beasts.

—UNKNOWN

Learn to play bad golf well.

—UNKNOWN

Reality is the leading cause of stress for those in touch with it.

—LILY TOMLIN

A bore is someone who opens his mouth and puts his feet in it.

—HENRY FORD

Only a fool tests the depth of the water with both feet.

—AFRICAN PROVERB

A habit is something you can do without thinking, which is why most of us have so many of them.

—FRANK CLARK

The lucky sperm club.

—MIKE THOMAS

Nailing Jell-O to a tree.

—UNKNOWN

Juggling cotton balls in a wind storm.

—Unknown

Golf is the only sport where the most feared opponent is yourself.

—Unknown

Golf can best be defined as an endless series of tragedies obscured by the occasional miracle.

—Unknown

If you see a turtle sitting on the top of a fence post, you know he had help getting there.

—Unknown

Americans always do the right thing after they have exhausted all other alternatives.

—Winston Churchill

The odds are good, but the goods are odd!

—About Alaskan Men

I live by a man's code, designed to fit a man's world, yet at the same time I never forget that a woman's first job is to choose the right shade of lipstick.

—Carole Lombard

Good judgment comes from experience, which generally comes from a lack of good judgment.

—Unknown

The Pruitt Approach—A Coyote Mentality

Going faster when you're lost doesn't help one bit.

—Unknown

Take your time and you only have to pull the trigger once.

—Unknown

Don't spur until you know which way you're going.

—Unknown

Timing has a lot to do with the success of a rain dance.

—Unknown

To err is human. To admit it, superhuman.

—Unknown

Nothing is so good as it seems beforehand.

—George Eliot

The hardest part about dieting is not watching what you eat; it's watching what other people eat.

—Unknown

Get your giggles and then give me advice.

—Unknown

I went up there and used an old negotiating tactic I've used often; I just begged them!

—David W. Pruitt

Humor

I am building a wealth creation engine of sorts, part-time.

—Unknown

It's raining soup, and I've got a fork.

—Unknown

It's good to be the king.

—The producers of Broadway Play

Smile—it's the second best thing you can do with your lips.

—Don Ward

The young know the rules, but the old know the exceptions.

—Oliver Wendell Holmes

You must not be afraid to lose in order to win.

—David W. Pruitt

Everything is funny as long as it's happening to someone else.

—Will Rogers

It's like getting up every morning and pushing the boulder up the hill. Usually you only get halfway up the hill and the boulder comes back down and crushes you.

—Robert Kosberg

It's hard to "piss" on someone, if he has you by the balls!

—Kirk Edelman

The Pruitt Approach—A Coyote Mentality

Last chance to go crazy.

—David W. Pruitt

If it was easy, the right Reverend Jessie Jackson would be doing it.

—David W. Pruitt

Get your facts first, and then you can distort them as much as you please.

—Mark Twain

Everybody is ignorant, only on different subjects.

—Will Rogers

Half our life is spent trying to find something to do with the time we have rushed through life trying to save.

—Will Rogers

What I need is a lawyer with enough juice to get Ray Charles a driver's license.

—Lenny Bruce

I believe that sex is one of the most beautiful, natural, wholesome things that money can buy.

—Tom Clancy

You know "that look" women get when they want sex? Me neither.

—Steve Martin

Humor

Women: can't live with them, can't live with them.

—JOHN PARKER

Having sex is like playing bridge. If you don't have a good partner, you'd better have a good hand.

—WOODY ALLEN

Bisexuality immediately doubles your chances for a date on Saturday night.

—RODNEY DANGERFIELD

There are a number of mechanical devices which increase sexual arousal, particularly in women. Chief among these is the Mercedes-Benz 500 SL.

—LYNN LAVNER

Leaving sex to the feminist is like letting your dog vacation at the taxidermist.

—MATT BARRY

Sex at age ninety is like trying to shoot pool with a rope.

—GEORGE BURNS

Sex is one of the nine reasons for reincarnation. The other eight are unimportant.

—GEORGE BURNS

Women might be able to fake orgasms, but men can fake whole relationships.

—SHARON STONE

The Pruitt Approach—A Coyote Mentality

My girlfriend always laughs during sex—no matter what she's reading.

—**Steve Jobs**
Founder, Apple Computers

Hockey is a sport for white men. Basketball is a sport for black men. Golf is a sport for white men dressed like black pimps.

—**Tiger Woods**

My mother never saw the irony in calling me a son of a bitch.

—**Jack Nicholson**

Clinton lied. A man might forget where he parks or where he lives, but he never forgets oral sex, no matter how bad it is.

—**Barbara Bush**
Former First Lady

Women need a reason to have sex. Men just need a place.

—**Billy Crystal**

Instead of getting married again, I'm going to find a woman I don't like and just give her a house!

—**Rod Stewart**

If you're going to do something tonight you'll be sorry for tomorrow morning, sleep late.

—**Henny Youngman**

I'd give up chocolate, but I am no quitter.

—Unknown

Life's tough. It's even tougher if you're stupid.

—John Wayne

A clear conscience usually is a sign of a poor memory.

—Terry Bradshaw

Don't argue with an idiot; people watching may not be able to tell the difference.

—Unknown

I have taken more from alcohol than alcohol has taken from me.

—Winston Churchill

I drink to make other people more interesting.

—Ernest Hemingway

Money isn't everything, but it sure keeps the kids in touch!

—Unknown

If money can fix it, it ain't a problem.

—David W. Pruitt

For financial reasons alone, money is better than the lack thereof.

—Unknown

The Pruitt Approach—A Coyote Mentality

If I agreed with you, we'd both be wrong.

—UNKNOWN

To steal ideas from one person is plagiarism. To steal from many is research.

—UNKNOWN

A clear conscience is the sign of a fuzzy memory.

—UNKNOWN

Only two things are infinite, the universe and human stupidity.

—ALBERT EINSTEIN

They ain't nothing he can't fix with WD-40 and a crescent wrench—made in America.

—TOBY KEITH

I'm a hay seed, plow boy, farm kid, and a cowboy.

—TOBY KEITH

I don't recognize anyone here I don't know.

—DAVID W. PRUITT

I can eat from road kill to vegetarian.

—DAVID W. PRUITT

Humor

I feel like a ninth grader: horny, healthy, with no worries or fears.

—**David W. Pruitt**
(66 years old)

Golf is an easy game but hard to play.

—**Tiger Woods**

You can never get enough of what you don't really need.

—**Unknown**

You are going to get older, but you don't have to get old.

—**George Burns**
(100 years old)

You should give your kids enough money so they can do something, but not enough for them to do nothing.

—**George Clooney**

Resentment is like drinking poison and hoping it will kill your enemy.

—**Nelson Mandela**

This is the place where brilliant minds assemble to willfully pool ignorance with questionable logic in order to reach unlikely conclusions.

— **A sign presented to JoAnn Brisco**
Owner, Jo Jo's Eatery, Midland, Texas

Forgive your enemies, but remember their names.

—Unknown

Money cannot buy happiness, but it's more comfortable to cry in a Mercedes than on a bicycle.

—Unknown

Help someone when they are in trouble and they will remember you when they're in trouble again.

—Unknown

Many people are alive only because it's illegal to shoot them.

—Unknown

All the happiness in the world cannot buy you money.

—Toby Keith

I am a man of simple tastes, easily satisfied with the best.

—Winston Churchill

Stage Night

Paleolithic

Drink deep to Uncle Uglug
That early heroic human
The first to eat an oyster
The first to marry a woman.

God's curse on him who murmurs.
As the banquet wares moisten

Had only he eaten the woman.
Had only he married the oyster.

—**Ogden Nash**

She blinked him away.

—**Pat Pruitt**

I hesitate to articulate for fear of deviating from the direct paths of rectitude.

—**Joe E. Kerr**

The only time people dislike gossip is when you gossip about them.

—**Will Rogers**

If you want a baby, have a new one, don't baby the old one.

—**Jessamyn West**

Golf is a good walk spoiled.

—**Mark Twain**

A dog never forgets where he buried his bone.

—**Unknown**

Stuff tends to break when it's loaned or borrowed.

—**Unknown**

Don't share a crosscut saw with a quitter.

—**Unknown**

The Pruitt Approach—A Coyote Mentality

Man is the only animal that blushes or needs to.

—MARK TWAIN

The principle difference between a cat and a lie is that a cat only has nine lives.

—MARK TWAIN

Never ask a lawyer to draft a contract and to defend that contract.

—UNKNOWN

There are three kinds of lies—lies, damned lies, and statistics.

—MARK TWAIN

Girlie good.

—DAVID W. PRUITT

Sadder than a one car funeral.

—UNKNOWN

When it's third and ten, you can have the milk drinkers; I'll take the whiskey drinkers every time.

—MAX MCGEE
Green Bay Packers receiver

I found that it's not good to talk about my troubles. Eighty percent of the people who hear them don't care and the other twenty percent are glad you're having them.

—TOMMY LASORDA
LA Dodgers manager

Humor

I learned a long time ago that 'minor surgery' is when they do the operation on someone else, not you.

—**Bill Walton**
Portland Trail Blazers

If we got one tenth of what was promised to us in these State of the Union speeches, there wouldn't be any inducement to go to heaven.

—**Will Rogers**

ATTITUDE

RALPH WALDO EMERSON

Nothing great was ever achieved without enthusiasm.

The Pruitt Approach—A Coyote Mentality

Reframing obstacles is key to turning problems (obstacles) into opportunities.

—Unknown

Optimism is a happiness magnet.

—Mary Lou Retton

If your vision is right, you'll win.

—Unknown

If it's your dream and passion, you will not question stretching way outside your comfort zone. Without going beyond, you'll be where you are—years from now.

—Unknown

It's simple but not easy.

—David W. Pruitt

There are no victories at discount prices.

—Ike Eisenhower

Do right and risk the consequences.

—Sam Houston

He who never made a mistake never made a discovery.

—Samuel Smiles

Impossible takes a little longer.

—Unknown

Attitude

What we see depends mainly on what we look for.

—Unknown

Seek first to understand, then to be understood.

—Unknown

Attitudes are more important than facts.

—Norman Vincent Peale

Hunt reasons to say thank you.

—David W. Pruitt

I seldom know answers but never in doubt.

—Michael McKinney

Nothing is so bad that it might have been worse.

—Unknown

The only ability I might have is the ability to overcome a bad lunch.

—Unknown

If I always do what I've always done, I'll always get what I've already got.

—Unknown

Ask not how many the enemy are, but where they are.

—Unknown

The Pruitt Approach—A Coyote Mentality

Never complain, never explain.

—Unknown

My attitude has always been, if it's worth playing, it's worth paying the price to win.

—Paul "Bear" Bryant

Although risk takers thrive on risks, they don't take chances.

—Robert J. Kriegel

You don't say whoa in a horse race.

—Unknown

The things which matter most must never be at the mercy of the things which matter least.

—Goethe

Attitude is contagious; what are you passing around?

—Connie Ladd

Swiped with pride from the best.

—Tom Peters

Attitude of gratitude.

—Unknown

It's hard to bring newness to order.

—Earl Nightingale

Attitude

Do you want to be right or happy?

—Unknown

The measure of a man is the way he bears up under misfortune.

—Plutarch

Self-help must precede help from others.

—Morarji Desai

Don't pay for safety; it's the most dangerous thing in the world.

—Hugh Walpole

See everything; overlook a great deal; correct a little.

—Pope John Paul XXII

I've experienced many troubles and some have actually come true.

—Mark Twain

Self-pity in its early stages is as snug as a feather mattress. Only when it hardens does it become uncomfortable.

—Maya Angelou

How many cares one loses when one decides not to be something but to be someone.

—Coco Chanel

Consider that this day never dawns again.

—**Dante**

The butterfly counts not months but moments and yet has time enough.

—**Rabindranath Tagore**

Circumstances are like a feather bed: comfortable if you are on top, but smothering if you are underneath.

—**Anonymous**

No one can make you feel inferior without your consent.

—**Eleanor Roosevelt**

Most people are about as happy as they make their minds to be.

—**Abraham Lincoln**

There is a majesty in simplicity.

—**Alexander Pope**

True strength is delicate.

—**Louise Nevelson**

The worse a situation becomes, the less it takes to turn it around and the bigger the upside.

—**George Soros**

Attitude

Stay hungry, stay foolish.

—STEWARD BRAND

The good things of prosperity are to be wished, but the good things that belong to adversity are to be admired.

—SENECA

What is right is not always popular and what is popular is not always right.

—ALBERT EINSTEIN

The real act of discovery consists not in finding new lands but in seeing with new eyes.

—MARCEL PROUST

Bad stuff is always easier to believe.

—DAVID W. PRUITT

You have to have a darkness for the dawn to come.

—HARRISON FORD

It doesn't take a very big man to carry a grudge.

—UNKNOWN

Forgive your enemies; it messes with their head.

—UNKNOWN

The Pruitt Approach—A Coyote Mentality

Most of the stuff folks worry about never happens, but stuff they don't worry about does, so we worry about the right amount but about the wrong things.

—DAVID W. PRUITT

The easiest thing to do in the world is to neglect the important and give in to the urgent.

—UNKNOWN

All would live long, but none would be old. He is young enough who has health, but he is rich enough who has no debts.

—UNKNOWN

To know the road ahead, ask those who are coming back on the road.

—CHINESE PROVERB

The young man who has not wept is a savage, and the old man who will not laugh is a fool.

—GEORGE SANTAYANA

Quantum growth eliminates clear sailing. So you'd better learn to navigate troubled waters.

—UNKNOWN

If you have no destination, wherever you end up will be acceptable.

—UNKNOWN

Patience is just an excuse for procrastination.

—UNKNOWN

Attitude

Not everything that counts can be counted. And not everything that can be counted counts.

—ALBERT EINSTEIN

Comparisons give us cancer of the soul.

—UNKNOWN

Do the right thing and do it right.

—LUIS GONZALES

Not only do what's right, but what you should do!

—DAVID W. PRUITT

Speak of the other person as if he is always present.

—STEPHEN COVEY

You can't control events, but you can use these events to your advantage.

—UNKNOWN

You can't build a reputation on what you are going to do.

—HENRY FORD

When your values are clear to you, making decisions becomes easier.

—ROY DISNEY

The consequences of a misguided decision is de minimis in the cosmos of eternity.

—UNKNOWN

The Pruitt Approach—A Coyote Mentality

You will not always have all the answers. Take seriously the advice of only those you greatly respect.

—UNKNOWN

The only difference between a champ and a chump is the "u."

—UNKNOWN

Get ruthless about trying something different.

—UNKNOWN

Set goals you cannot achieve in your lifetime.

—UNKNOWN

You cannot grow exponentially by yourself. You need the support of others.

—UNKNOWN

The only things in this life that you'll really regret are the risks and adventures you didn't take.

—UNKNOWN

People with low self-esteem protect themselves by not taking risks. High self-esteem gives you the power of confidence to take chances.

—UNKNOWN

Your doubts are not the product of accurate thinking but of habitual thinking.

—UNKNOWN

= Attitude =

SEVEN THINGS THAT WILL DESTROY US

Politics without principle
Pleasure without conscience
Wealth without work
Knowledge without character
Business without morality
Science without humanity
Worship without sacrifice

—MOHANDAS K. GANDHI

ALL PURPOSE WARNING

Living is intrinsically hazardous, which is why you are going to die, sooner or later.

You can make your existence more dangerous than it has to be by doing stupid things.
This company is not your mommy; despite the honeyed lies of politicians, neither is the government. You are responsible for your actions.

—RUSTY JONES
1996

WORRY BUSTER

Write it down.
Worst case scenario.
Resolve to accept the worst case.
Immediately start improving on worst case scenario.

—UNKNOWN

THE STORY OF TWO FROGS

Once upon a time, there was a frog who was dropped into a pot of hot water. Feeling the intense heat, he immediately jumped out and saved his life. But there was another frog who was put into a pot of cold water and sat on a burner over the low heat. One degree at a time the temperature increased, but the frog became accustomed to it, stayed in the pot, and eventually boiled.

—UNKNOWN

Worry is like a rocking chair, it gives you something to do, but it doesn't get you anywhere.

—UNKNOWN

Be not afraid of life. Believe that life is worth living, and your belief will help create the fact.

—HENRY JAMES

A real home is a shelter from the storms of life, a place to enjoy, a place in which to relax, a place of peace and rest. A true home is the center of all human hopes and ideals. It does not have to be a mansion.

—DR. CLIFFORD R. ANDERSON

He who establishes his argument by noise and command shows that his reason is weak.

—MONTAIGNE

With all thy getting get understanding.

—PROVERBS 4:7

Attitude

Confidence is the companion of success.

—Unknown

You may succeed when others do not believe in you, but you never succeed when you do not believe in yourself.

—Unknown

It is neither wealth nor splendor, but tranquility and occupation which give happiness.

—Thomas Jefferson

Self-conquest is the greatest of victories.

—Plato

A small trouble is like a pebble. Hold it close to your eye, and it fills the whole world and puts everything out of focus. Hold it at a proper viewpoint, and it can be examined and properly classified. Throw it at your feet, and it can be seen in its true setting, just one more tiny bump on the pathway to eternity.

—Unknown

Don't wear your wishbone where your backbone ought to be.

—Elizabeth Gilbert

There's a lot to see if you keep your head up.

—Unknown

The Pruitt Approach—A Coyote Mentality

Sympathy is never wasted except when you give it to yourself.

—JOHN DRAPER

I find the great thing in this world is not so much where we stand, as in what direction we are moving . . .

—OLIVER WENDELL HOLMES

Courage consists not in blindly overlooking danger but in seeing it and conquering it.

—JEAN PAUL FRIEDRICH RICHTER

Superior people talk about ideas, average people talk about things, and little people talk about other people.

—UNKNOWN

If you expect your vacuum sweeper to pick up golf balls, you will be disappointed.

—DR. JAY MCSPADEN

I'm an imperfect perfectionist.

—DAVID W. PRUITT

No one has ever died because he was kicked in the "balls."

—DAVID W. PRUITT

We are all mortal until the first kiss and the second glass of wine.

—EDWARD GALEANO

Attitude

He has the ability to "powder the pig."

—**Denny Bartell**
About Wildcatter Van Dyke of Houston

I've been fortunate that those who choose to be my enemy have all been idiots.

—**David W. Pruitt**

One evening an Indian told his son about a battle that goes on inside of people. He said, "My son, the battle is between two wolves. One is evil. It is anger, envy, sorrow, regret, greed, arrogance, self-pity, guilt, resentment, inferiority, lies, false pride, and ego. The other is good. It is joy, peace, love, hope, serenity, humility, kindness, benevolence, empathy, generosity, truth, compassion, and faith." The son thought about it for a moment and asked, "Which wolf wins?" His father simply said, "The one you feed."

—**Unknown**

Treat others as gentlemen, not that they are but because you are.

—**Unknown**

The first step to solve any problem is you have to defeat yourself before you defeat someone else.

—**Mike Leach**
Football Head Coach, TTU

Any problem is solvable if you allow yourself the clear-mindedness to find the solution.

—**Mike Leach**
Football Head Coach, TTU

The Pruitt Approach—A Coyote Mentality

I'd rather live a day with the lions than live a thousand years with the lambs.

—**An American Soldier in Iraq**

Age is an issue of mind over matter. If you don't mind, it doesn't matter.

—**Mark Twain**

A little bit older, a whole lot bolder.

—**Unknown**

Happiness is not a matter of good fortune or worldly possessions. It's a mental attitude. It comes from appreciating what we have, instead of being miserable about what we don't have. It's so simple yet so hard for the human mind to comprehend.

—**Unknown**

Whatever you do, work at it with all your heart.

—**Colossians 3:23**
(Ryan Tannehill, Miami Dolphins and Texas A&M Quarterback Puts This on Autographs.)

If the activity you are engaged in is, in your judgment, important, if you are central to it and if you are doing it with people you respect and can learn from and people you enjoy working with, then you have a formula for happiness and probably achievement because you will very likely put an awful lot more of yourself into it.

—**Donald Rumsfeld**
Secretary of Defense

Attitude

Whatever you can do or dream you can, begin it. Boldness has genius, power, and magic in it.

—Goethe

Knowledge is realizing that the street is one way; wisdom is looking in both directions anyway.

—Unknown

Nothing is impossible when we follow our inner guidance even when its direction may threaten us by reversing our usual logic.

—Gerald Jampolsky

It's sometimes better to have balls bigger than your brain.

—David W. Pruitt
(My thoughts on deciding I would take the jury decision vs. the district attorney's plea bargain of manslaughter August 21, 2010. Verdict: not guilty! I set the alarm after the trial ended for an early Saturday flight, and it went off before we got to bed.)

When you are fighting a gorilla, you first hit him as hard as you can in the mouth.

—Jimmy Johnson
Former Coach, Dallas Cowboys

They will forget what you said, but they will never forget how you made them feel.

—Carl W. Buechner

The Pruitt Approach—A Coyote Mentality

Much reading is an oppression of the mind and extinguishes the natural candle, which is the reason of so many senseless scholars in the world.

—WILLIAM PENN

Any friend of my enemy is my enemy.

—ARABIC PROVERB

Laughter is an instant vacation.

—MILTON BERLE

When asked what he thought about when he struck out, Babe Ruth said, "I think about hitting home runs."

—UNKNOWN

You don't ask for the butcher's recipe for sausage, there's nothing in it that will kill you.

—DAVID W. PRUITT

TEXAS

David W. Pruitt

I was born and bred and proud to be a native Texan. My family is a fourth generation—close to 130 years—Texan. Seldom do others not like it here. There is something for all. As the bumper sticker goes, "I'm not a native Texan, but I got here as soon as I could."

Never forget, son, when you represent Texas, always go first class.

—James Michener

I'll keep us out of war with Oklahoma.

—Kinky Freidman
A campaign-for-governor promise

Some folks look at me and see a certain swagger, which in Texas is called "walking."

—George W. Bush

Texas could get along without the United States, but the United States cannot, except at great hazard, exist without Texas.

—Sam Houston

There's a vastness here, and Texans breathe that vastness into their soul. They dream big dreams and think big thoughts because there is nothing to hem them in.

—Conrad Hilton

Texas is a great state. It's the "old man river" of states. No matter who runs it or what happens to it politically, it just keeps rolling along.

—Will Rogers

Tom Landry is a perfectionist. If he was married to Racquel Welch, he'd expect her to cook.

—Don Meredith

Attitude

I have said that Texas is a state of mind; but I think it is more than that. It is a mystique closely approximating a religion.
—John Steinbeck

I'd rather be a fencepost in Texas than the king of Tennessee.
—Chris Wall

At Odessa we became Texans and proud of it.
—George H. W. Bush

A West Texas rain: a sandstorm.
—Boyce House

Give me an army of West Point graduates and I'll win a battle; give me a handful of Texas Aggies, and I'll win a war!
—General George S. Patton

The weather in Texas shows that God has a sense of humor.
—Anonymous

Vote early and vote often. That's the way we do it in Texas.
—Barbara Bush

The enemy never sees the backs of my Texans!
—Robert E. Lee

All new states are invested, more or less, by a class of noisy second-rate men who are always in favor of rash and extreme measures. But Texas was absolutely overrun by such men.

—Sam Houston

We find some West Texans are Eastern prejudiced.

—BARBARA BUSH

Good thing we've got politics in Texas—finest form of free entertainment ever invented.

—MOLLY IVINS

Texans for the most part have never learned how to be dull.

—RANDOLPH B. CAMPBELL

You can always tell a Texan, but you can't tell him much.

—ANONYMOUS

A politician is a fellow who will lay down your life for his country.

—TEXAS GUINAN

Oil rich boys had a nice, sweet smile, but when you finished meeting with them, your socks were missing and you hadn't even noticed they'd taken your boots.

—LARRY HAGMAN

He's nothing but a damn vegetarian. . . .

—SAM HOUSTON
(Dismissing a political rival)

If Texas were a sane place, it wouldn't be nearly as much fun.

—MOLLY IVINS

= Attitude =

There were men in Texas whom I would not have cared to meet in a secluded place.

—Ulysses S. Grant
(During the Mexican War)

How can you look at the Texas legislature and still believe in intelligent design?

—Kinky Friedman

Texans made their noisiest money in oil and that's something like winning it in a crap game.

—Harlan Miller

I am forced to conclude that God made Texas on his day off for pure entertainment, just to prove that all that diversity could be crammed into one section of earth by a really top hand.

—Mary Lasswell

Govern wisely, and as little as possible.

—Sam Houston

If English was good enough for Jesus Christ, it's good enough for me.

—Unknown

It wasn't till I left Texas that I realized creeks had water in them.

—Beverly Hogan

The Pruitt Approach—A Coyote Mentality

I support gay marriage. I believe they have a right to be as miserable as the rest of us.

—Kinky Friedman

Van Horn, Texas, is too healthy; we had to shoot a man to start a cemetery.

—Bill Goynes

In Texas, everything is bigger. When Texans win, they win big, and when they lose, it's spectacular.

—Robert Kiyosaki

Texas is a blend of valor and swagger.

—Carl Sandburg

Anybody who wanders around the world saying, "Hell yes, I'm from Texas" deserves whatever happens to him.

—Hunter S. Thompson

Don't mess with Texas.

—Texas Department of Transportation slogan

Texas is neither southern nor western. Texas is Texas.

—William Blakely

The town which can't support one lawyer can always support two lawyers.

—Lyndon B. Johnson

Attitude

In the Panhandle, we like to call Route 66 the mother road because everybody just kinda fled to the road, hoping the road would take them to better times and better things in their life.

—DELBERT TREW

Ask any Texan from Dalhart to Brownsville to describe Texas food, and you'll get as many answers as there are miles (or armadillos) between two cities.

—STEPHAN PYLES

My favorite Aggie joke? I'm sorry. I don't understand the question.

—LYLE LOVETT

There's a saying in Big Spring: No, this isn't the end of the earth, but you can see it from here.

—STEPHAN PYLES

I think Texans have more fun than the rest of the world.

—TOMMY TUNE

That's why I like Texans so much. They took a great failure [like the Alamo] and turned it into a tourist destination that makes them millions.

—ROBERT KIYOSAKI

I never saw a creek with water in it until I moved out of Texas.

—KINKY FRIEDMAN

The Pruitt Approach—A Coyote Mentality

To make something happen, tell a Texan it can't be done.

—UNKNOWN

In England, it's called a pound; in Hereford, a pound is called money.

—BILLBOARD ENTERING HEREFORD,
Texas, 2013

Almost everything about Texas reveals some trademark of an iron will.

—TRACY LARSON

The film looks suspiciously like the game itself.

—BURN PHILLIPS
New Orleans Saints, after viewing a lopsided loss to the Atlanta Falcons

We were tipping off our plays. Whenever we broke from the huddle, three backs were laughing and one was pale as a ghost.

—JOHN BREEN
Houston Oilers

We kept tipping off our plays—because whoever was to carry the football was wearing the helmet.

—RONNIE FLOWERS
Guthrie, TX, football star player

Attitude

I don't know. I only played there for nine years.

—**WALT GARRISON**
Dallas Cowboys fullback when asked if Tom Landry ever smiles

LOVE

Rev. Henri Nouwen

Hope and faith will both come to an end when we die. But love will remain. Love is eternal. Love comes from God and returns to God. When we die, we will lose everything that life gave us except love. The love with which we lived our lives is the life of God within us. It is the divine, indestructable core of our being. This love not only will remain but will bear fruit from generation to generation.

LOVE

Appendix

Pruitt's First, or Near-Firsts, in the Electric Utility Business

Even though these were valuable contributions by Pruitt to the electric utility industry, don't look for him to be in any Hall of Fame.

1. First and only electric cooperative to have a director who later became United States Secretary of Commerce
2. First electric distribution cooperative to own its own natural gas supply for producing electricity at a cost hedge for wholesale electric power cost to its customers
3. New three and single-phase electric line design
4. First to merge electric cooperatives in Texas with two separate PUC-approved sets of electric rates
5. First to merge in Texas non-contiguous
6. No inventory
7. First electric cooperative in Texas to use automated meter reading
8. First to go public from being an electric (mutual) cooperative
9. First to go public to private with a 62 percent stock premium to stockholders
10. First to lease entire vehicle fleet instead of owning them

The Pruitt Approach—A Coyote Mentality

11. First cooperative to move headquarters to large city

12. First cooperative to start an insurance company—Offshore Captive

13. First utility to totally outsource IT—Delinea

14. First utility to set up electrician company to work behind any electric utility's meter

15. First cooperative to adjust PCRF and depreciation to catch up to current billing cycle, which picked up $3.5 million

16. First cooperative with CFC Bank to utilize $38 million line of credit then roll over to long-term capital financing to help tier with CFC approval

17. First to sell satellite TV services under company's name without using the capital to start or run the company contracted to sell or install

18. First cooperative or IOU to own natural gas pipeline-gathering system

19. First utility to own and operate commercial building-management company

20. First utility to own a royalty oil and natural gas company—Map Resources

21. Built most transmission line (305 miles in Texas) during 1990s. First to build it customer's (landowner's) way (route). Avoided lawsuits; engineers had to build our way instead of theirs. Now this is the standard utility method of picking routes for expansion of electric lines

Appendix

22. First utility in the nation in the eighties to have advertising and information instead of music on telephone hold

23. First to sell insurance for customer's equipment agreement. Lighting etc. set $75,000 as company's deductible-cut insurance cost

24. First electric company in the nation to drop defined benefit without cutting dedicated dollars to employee's retirement 12.5 percent contribution. Had all employees sign agreement within twenty-four hours of proposal

25. First wholesale customer of IOU to cancel long-term wholesale power contract and attempt to wheel power over IOU, TXU's line from CoGen power plant (400 miles)—no wheeling PUC rules back then

26. First electric company in the nation to use one-man buckets with a one-man crew in rural areas. Let linemen troubleshooters set all rules. This cut operating costs by 20 percent

27. Pruitt was the highest paid electric cooperative employee ever over his total career

28. First in Texas electric company to offer automatic membership to self-owner member credit union

29. First in the early nineties to use customer committee with authority and power to set retail electric rates for all rate classes, with PUC final approval

30. Transmission material, totaling over $16 million, purchased before had PUC authority to build 305 miles of transmission line to expedite construction completion

31. First electric wires utility to establish a telecom subsidiary company to acquire existing landline-based telecom utilities

INDEX

A

Adams, Bob 37, 48, 119, 131, 134, 162
Aesculapius of Thessaly 40
Alaskan Men 177
Alcoholics Anonymous 6
Alcott, Louisa May 148
Ali, Mohammed 1
Allen, James 13
Allen, Jeff 166
Allen, Woody 113, 181
American Soldier 206
Amos, Wally 75
Anderson, Clifford R. 202
Angelou, Maya 195
Anonymous 3, 18, 23-25, 29, 31-33, 50, 80, 97, 114, 123, 137, 139, 147, 151, 152, 164, 173, 174, 196, 211, 212
Arend, John 154
Aristotle 27, 36, 80
Arnold, Oren 129
Arnold, Stanley 51
Ashbrook, Tom 95
Askenberg, J. 147
Astley, Jacob 9
Augustine, St. 145
Aurelius, Marcus 24, 26

B

Bagehot, Walter 106
Bailey, Philip James 53
Ball, Lucille 172

Balzac, Honore 165
Barker, Joel 44
Barry, Matt 181
Barrymore, Ethel 54
Bartell, Denny 205
Barton, Bruce 112
Beck, Martha 7
Beecher, Henry Ward 16, 139
Ben-Gurion, David 32
Bennett, Arnold 30
Berle, Milton 208
Berra, Yogi 155, 167, 168
Bibesco, Elizabeth 10
Biggers, Earl Derr 175
Billboard
    Hereford, Texas 216
Billings, Josh 57
Blake, James 43
Blakely, William 214
Blankship, Herb 165
Bombeck, Erma 172
Bonaparte, Napoleon 37, 40, 138
Borge, Victor 168
Boring, Mac 4
Bower, David W. 10
Bowie, Jim 5
Bradford, Alex 16
Bradley, Bill 129
Bradley, Tom 110
Bradshaw, Terry 183
Brand, Steward 197
Breen, John 216

Brisco, JoAnn
    Sign 185
Broadway Play, producers 179
Brotherton, Joseph 22
Brown H. Jackson, Jr. 39
Brown, Steve 150
Browning, Robert 13, 22
Bruce, Lenny 113, 180
Bryan, William Jennings 36
Bryant, Paul "Bear" 194
Buchwald, Art 57
Buechner, Carl W. 207
Bullock, Sandra 161
Burke, Edmund 56
Burns, Dan 100
Burns, George 172, 181, 185
Bush, Barbara 182, 211, 212
Bush, George H. W. 211
Bush, George W. 23, 210
Butler, Samuel 173
Butterworth, Eric 10

C

Cain, Herman 149
Campbell, Randolph B. 212
Capacchione, Lucia 57
Carlin, George 173
Carlyle, Thomas 78, 79
Carnegie, Dale 45, 88, 156
Carter, Bob 105
Carter, Johnny 115, 116
Cato the Elder 15
CFC 20
Chanel, Coco 195

Chapin, Henry D. 25
Charron, Pierre 23
2 Chronicles 7:14 19
Churchill, Randolph 106
Churchill, Winston 88, 110, 116, 123, 159, 162, 165, 177, 183, 186
Clancy, Tom 180
Clark, Fred A. 158
Clark, Frank 176
Clarke, Arthur C. 26
Cleveland, Grover 69
Clinton, Ronnie Wayne 107, 108
Clooney, George 185
Colette 34, 174
Collier, Robert 27, 122, 147
Collins, James C. 49
Collins, Marva 110
Colossians 3:23 206
Confucius 40-42, 54, 136
Cooley, Charles Horton 42
Coolidge, Calvin 112
Coonradt, Chuck 97
Corbett, James J. 136
Courtney, Henry A. 127
Covey, Stephen 74, 119, 199
Crabbe, George 28
Crawford, Joan 58
Cromwell, Oliver 124
Crowell, Grace Noll 2
Crockett, Davy 25, 141
Crystal, Billy 182
Cummings, Allan 131

D

D'amato, Constantine 83
Dana, John Cotton 53, 140
Dana, Richard Henry 53, 140
Dangerfield, Rodney 181
Dante 196
Davis, Dick 94
Davis, Shelby 92
Davis, Stan 107
De La Bruyere, Jean 4
De La Fontaine, Jean 138
De La Rochefoucauld, François 56
De Montherlant, Henri 23
Desai, Morarji 195
De Sales, St. Francis 31
Deuteronomy 8:17-18 17
Dickens, Charles 23
Dirksen, Everett 70
Disney, Roy 199
Douglas, Mack R. 147
Draper, John 204
Drucker, Peter 48, 96, 99, 121, 166
Dumas, Alexandre 3, 78

E

Edelman, Kirk 179
Edison, Thomas A. 115, 150
Einstein, Albert 11, 34, 119, 135, 141, 155, 169, 184, 197, 199
Eisenhower, Ike 192
Eliot, George 151, 178
Eliot, T. S. 49, 112, 149
Elliston, George 30

Emerson, Ralph Waldo 3, 24, 34, 35, 96, 191
Esar, Evan 56
Ewing, Sam 57

F

Fama, Eugene 106
Feather, William 123
Fields, J. 114
Flagg, Fannie 173
Flowers, Ronnie 216
Fonteyn, Margot 93
Forbes, Malcolm 88, 123
Forbes, Steve 64-69, 130
Ford, Harrison 197
Ford, Henry 46, 54, 75, 88, 128, 148, 157, 176, 199
Francis of Assisi, St. 144
Franklin, Benjamin 4, 16, 31, 37, 38, 103, 108, 115, 129, 161
Friedman, Kinky 210, 213-15
Fredrick, Pauline 89
Frost, Robert 163
Fuller, Thomas 34

G

Galeano, Edward 204
Gallagher, Robert C. 86
Gandhi, Mohandas K. 19, 201
Garland, Judy 171
Garrett, Jason 145
Garretty, Marion C. 146
Garrison, Walt 217
Garza, Sonny 99
Gaskett, Elizabeth 44

Gates, Bill 129, 140, 155
Gavin, Norm 98, 131
Giants, New York
    Locker Room Board 175
Gilbert, Elizabeth 203
Gilbert, Rob 124
Gilpin, Bernard 139
Glaser, Edward 107
Glover, Jerry 130
Goethe 24, 25, 29, 194, 207
Gonzales, Luis 199
Goynes, Bill 214
Graham, Billy 12
Grant, Micki 16
Grant, Ulysses S. 213
Grenfell, Wilfred T. 33
Gretzsky, Wayne 48, 153
Guinan, Texas 212
Gumble, Bryant 164

H

Habib, Ed 4
Hagman, Larry 212
Haldane, John 16
Halifax, Charles Lindley Wood 15
Hampton, Lionel 32
Hannibal 110
Hazlitt, William 59, 70
Helps, Arthur 29
Hemingway, Ernest 183
Henley, Linda 36
Herbert, George 114
Heywood, Thomas 151

Hibbard, Richard R. 47
Hill, Napoleon 75, 112
Hillis, Burton 36
Hilton, Conrad 210
Hodges, Clarence E. 159
Hogan, Beverly 213
Holland, Josiah Gilbert 12, 30, 36
Holmes, Oliver Wendell 3, 34, 179, 204
Holts, Lou 37
Hooker, Richard 87
Horace 31
House, Boyce 211
House Judiciary Committee 18
Houston, Sam 192, 210-13
Hubbard, Elbert 53, 54, 56, 79, 148
Huckley, Thomas 150
Hummel, Charles 97
Hunt, H. L. 93
Huxley, Thomas Henry 137
Hymn, Methodist 14

I

Icahn, Carl 57
Irving, Washington 151
Ivins, Molly 212

J

Jackson, Phil 116, 127
Jamail, Joe 79
James, Bill 92, 94
James, Henry 38, 202
James, Lebron 73
James, William 158

Jamplosky, Gerard 207
Jay, John 19
Jefferson, Thomas 19, 56, 64-67, 139
Jobs, Steve 98, 109, 138, 145, 182
John Paul XXII, Pope 195
Johnson, Jimmy 161, 167, 207
Johnson, Lyndon B. 153, 214
Johnson, Samuel 33, 52, 110
Johnson, Spencer 82
Jones, Franklin P. 6
Jones, Jerry 125
Jones, Rusty 201
Jones, Thomas 62
Jonson, Ben 15
Jordan, Michael 118
Joshua 24:15 16

K

Kaiser, Kurt 14
Kallback, Gary 113
Keith, Toby 184, 186
Keller, Helen 30, 44, 135, 151
Kelvin, William Thomson 70
Kennedy, John F. 41, 50, 76, 77, 83
Kennedy John F., II 36
Kennedy, Robert F. 28
Kennevan, Walter J. 167
Kent, Corita 157
Kerr, Joe E. 187
Keynes, John Manard 106
Kezer, Pauline 149
Kipling, Rudyard 31, 33
Kiyosaki, Robert 214, 215

Knell, Sandra 61
Knoll, Chuck 126
Koran 15
Korda, Michael 128
Kosberg, Robert 42, 179
Kriegel, Robert J. 96, 97, 194
Kroc, Ray 122
Krzyzewski, Mike 102, 103
Kwong, Roshi 45

L

Ladd, Connie 194
Ladd, Jack D. 161
Lamb, Charles 98
Landers, Ann 154
Larson, Tracy 216
LaSorda, Tommy 188
Lasswell, Mary 213
Lauder, Estee 117
Lauer, Charles S. 133
Lavner, Lynn 181
LCRA Chairman 50
Leach, Mike 205
Lee, Bruce 143
Lee, Robert E. 211
Lehman Brothers 107
Leonard, Sugar Ray 147
Lerner, Al 59
Levenson, Sam 164
Liberty, Joe 92
Lincoln, Abraham 10, 25, 141, 146, 152, 196
Lombard, Carole 177
Lombardi, Vince 91, 94, 158

Longfellow, Henry Wadsworth 158
Lovett, Lyle 215
Lowell, James Russell 29

M

Mabie, Hamilton Wright 149
Macaulay 160
MacDonald, George 55, 127
Mackay, Harvey 43, 92, 175
Mackintosh, James 23
MacLaren, Alexander 29
Malloch, Douglas 62, 114
Mancuso, Joseph 104, 175
Mandela, Nelson 185
Mann, Horace 55
Mansfield, Katherine 78
Mantle, Mickey 164
Marin, Judith S. 40
Mark 11:24 9
Markova, Dawna 42
Marrs, Ross W. 22
Martin, Steve 180
Marx, Groucho 157, 167
Marshall, Peter 53
Maslow, Abraham 56
Matthew 6:33 8
May, Rollo 43
McCollum, Gordon 101
McCulloch, James Edward 76
McGee, Max 188
McKinney, Michael 193
McManus, Jean Kyler 2
Mclemore, Randy 14

McSpaden, Jay 204
Mears, Rick 148
Meglitsch, Paul A. 141
Melville, Herman 75
Menninger, Karl 22, 62
Meredith, Don 210
Meredith, George 28
Michener, James 210
Miller, Harlan 213
Miller, Johnny 162
Milliken, Robert A. 15, 70
Mingo, Jack 61
Modelle, Art 101
Moliere 151
Monson, Thomas 136
Montaigne 202
Moody, Dwight L. 139
Moore, George 115
Moos, N. H. 147
Morison, Elting E. 135
Morgan, Arthur E. 77
Mother Teresa 11, 13
Mulchay, Anne 105
Muller, Robert 34
Murray, Jim 171
Myers, David G. 51
Myrna, John 107

N

Namath, Joe 28
Nash, Ogden 171, 187
Navratilova, Martina 167
Nehru, Jawaharlal 82

Nevelson, Louise 196
Newman, Paul 172
Newton, Isaac 45
Nicholson, Jack 182
Nickerson, Steven Cash 62, 71, 108, 167
Nietzsche, Friedrich 24
Nightingale, Earl 44, 194
Nixon, Richard M. 45, 77
Nouwen, Rev. Henri 219
Nunes, Marianna 169, 170

O

Ortman, Mark 42

P

Palmer, George Herbert 35
Parker, John 181
Parker, Joseph 130
Pasteur, Louis 86
Paterno, Joe 89, 147
Patton, George S. 116, 152, 211
Pavese, Cesare 38
Peale, Norman Vincent 193
Pena, Dan 43, 49, 52, 57, 89, 98, 100, 123, 144
Pena, Linda 174
Penn, William 208
Perot, Ross 125
Perry, Rick 95
Peters, Tom 75, 194
Philippians 3:13-14 8
Philippians 4:13 8
Phillip II of Macedon 135
Phillips, Bob 142
Phillips, Burn 216

Picasso, Pablo 43
Pinero, Arthur Wing 30
Plank, Kevin 128
Plato 203
Plautus 25
Plutarch 195
Pope, Alexander 196
Porras, Jerry I. 49
Powell, Colin 103, 104
Prough, Ann 62
Proust, Marcel 197
Proverb
    African 176
    Arabic 208
    Buddhist 35
    Chinese 15, 55, 58, 131, 198
    English 60
    French 25
    German 35, 58
    Guatemalan 20
    Latin 115
    Iranian 24
    Irish 12, 27, 44
    Japanese 22, 147
    Scottish 4
    Swedish 32
    Yiddish 14
Proverbs 1:7 11
    4:7 202
    27:6 5
Pruitt, David W. ix-xiv, 2, 5, 19, 31, 38, 43, 51, 52, 76, 92-96, 98, 101, 104, 105, 110, 113, 114, 116, 118, 119, 122, 123, 127-29, 131, 136, 137, 139-42, 145, 146, 150, 155, 157,

160, 168, 171, 178-80, 183-85, 188, 192, 193, 197-99, 204, 205, 207-09, 219-22
Pruitt, Pat 28, 116, 187
Pruitt, Patricia R. 32
Psalm 16:11 8
   33:12a 19
   118:24 11
   136:1 9
Pyles, Stephan 215

Q

Quillen, Robert 11

R

Raisuli 59
Ramsey, Dave 92
Reagan, Ronald 63
Retton, Mary Lou 192
Reuven, Ron 161
Richter, Jean Paul Friedrich 204
Rickenbacker, Eddie 119
Rickover, Hyman 96
Robbins, Tony 87, 130, 162
Roche, Boyle 80
Rockefeller John D., Jr. 30
Rodriguez, Mark 107
Rogers, Will 46, 56, 60, 77, 168, 171, 179, 180, 187, 189, 210
Rohn, Jim 85
Rooney, Andy 172
Roosevelt, Eleanor 196
Roosevelt, Franklin D. 81, 142
Roosevelt, Theodore 52, 69, 75
Rothaus, Kelly Ann 33

Rowland, Helen 175
Rubin, Harriet 138
Rubin, Theodore 83
Rumsfeld, Donald 206
Ruskin, John 124
Russell, Bertrand 59
Russell, David 88
Ruth, Babe 161

S

Sandburg, Carl 214
Sanders, Deion 160
Santayana, George 198
Sartre, Jean-Paul 28
Saunders, Allen 61
Saxowsky, David 86
Schlossberg, Glenn 14, 44, 59, 80, 119, 125, 154
Schuller, Robert 152
Schutz, Peter 50, 137, 167
Schwarzenegger, Arnold 115
Schwertner, Ray 2
Scripps, E. W. 27
Seneca 35, 197
Shaw, George Bernard 77
Shay, R. E. 168
Sherman, John K. 54
Sherman, William T. 131
Sherrod, Blackie 59
Shinn, George 89
Shrontz, Frank 140
Sidney, Phillip 29, 34, 112
Sills, Beverly 50
Singletary, Bryan 108

Skelton, Red 172
Skilling, Jeff 77, 99, 103, 128
Smeltzer, Ruth 16
Smiles, Samuel 74, 192
Smith, Logan Persall 59
Smith, Sydney 118
Soros, George 196
Southard, John E. 55
Speaker, Tris 169
St. Johns, Adela Rogers 22
Stanley, Bessie Anderson 121
Steinbeck, John 61, 173, 211
Stengal, Casey 138
Stewart, Rod 182
Stone, Sharon 181
Story, Joseph 18
Stowe, Harriet Beecher 158
Strong, Patience 139
Suess, Dr. 159, 160
Sunday, Billy 75
Swindell, Sarah 35
Switzer, Barry 146
Syrus, Publilius 58

T

Tagore, Rabindranath 196
Tannehill, Ryan 206
Teasdale, Sara 40
Ten Boom, Corrie 9
Texas Department of Transportation 214
Thatcher, Margaret 99, 113
Thomas, Mike 176
Thompson, Hunter S. 214

Thoreau, Henry David 118, 161
Thurber, James 97
Thurow, Lester C. 86
Tinker, Grant 124
Tolstoy, Leo 86
Tomlin, Lily 174, 176
Tournier, Paul 83
Tracey, Bryan 89
Trew, Delbert 215
Trollope, Anthony 45
Truman, Harry S. 171
Trump, Donald 155
Tune, Tommy 215
Twain, Mark 3, 26, 36, 37, 41, 60, 83, 149, 153, 180, 187, 188, 195, 206

U

Unknown 3-5, 10-12, 14-18, 20, 21, 23, 25-27, 31, 32, 35, 37, 38, 40, 42-46, 48-58, 60-62, 64, 69, 70, 74, 76-80, 82, 83, 87-89, 92-102, 105-08, 110-14, 116, 118-23, 125-28, 130, 134-38, 140-41, 144-46, 148-57, 159-62, 164-66, 168-71, 173-79, 183-88, 192-95, 197, 198, 213, 216

V

Van Buren, Abigail 28
Van Gogh, Vincent 16
Vaughan, Norman 146
Voltaire 54
Von Clausewitz, Carl 115
Von Oech, Roger 157

W

Waitley, Denis 26, 35, 74, 79, 98, 111, 121, 124, 141
Wall, Chris 211
Walpole, Hugh 195
Walton, Bill 189
Walton, Izaak 9
Ward, Don 179
Warner, Harry M. 169
Washington, Booker T. 125
Wayland, H. L. 61
Wayne, John 183
    Headstone Inscription 38
Weinbaum, Dave 40
West, Jessamyn 166, 187
White, Stewart Edward 78
Wilde, Oscar 172
Williams, Robin 172
Wilnot, John 166
Wilson, Charles E. 148
Wilson, Woodrow 33
Winans, Vickie 13
Winfrey, Oprah 17
Winters, Shelly 165
Wooden, John 24, 57, 158
Woods, Tiger 182
Wright, Frank Lloyd 152

X

Y

Yanagidaira, Sakan 159
Youngman, Henny 182

Z

Zadra, Dan 159
Ziglar, Zig 136, 167

About the Author

David Ward Pruitt was born, bred, and raised on a dairy and beef cattle farm in northeast Texas. So it's obvious he learned to work early in life. Pruitt was a small-town athlete in Celeste, Texas. He was All-District in football and basketball. Later he was high point individual in the district track and field meet and was honored as Most Athletic Boy his senior year in high school.

David's "Daddy," as David and his sister, Jan, called their father, was the first to graduate from college in his family. He had both a bachelor's and a master's degree—a proud Texas Aggie. During World War II, David's Daddy, M. M. Pruitt, flew fifty missions over Hitler's oil fields in Polesti. He triple-dipped the Feds, retiring from the Air Force as a colonel, receiving social security and qualifying for an early retirement pension from the civil service for a physical disability. With the early disability from the Farmer's Home Administration (FMHA), he doubled the size of his dairy herd. He operated a dairy and beef cattle farm on about a section of land purchased from his father. Plus, he was area supervisor for the FMHA, commuting about sixty miles one way to his 8:00 to 5:00 job. This was after he had already done a full day's work on the farm before he left at 6:45 a.m.

His early disability retirement resulted from a hay bailing accident. On the Texas/Oklahoma football weekend in 1973, Pruitt got his leg cut off in a square press hay bailer and had to drive himself in a standard shift vehicle to get an ambulance to rush him to a Dallas hospital in the traffic of Texas/OU weekend. The accident happened as he unclogged the hay from the press—something David had done a thousand times but was just more lucky.

The Pruitt Approach—A Coyote Mentality

Then another freaky farm hay bailing accident happened to David's daddy about six years later. His left arm got lodged in a round hay bailer, and he was stuck in the bailer's two-thousand-pound rollers for over an hour. He finally realized he could free his arm by taking off his artificial leg and jamming it in the rollers. He then drove himself to his dairy and crashed the truck into the barn to get the attention of Willie, his milk hand, to drive him to the hospital in Greenville. Willie was a great black fellow who worked for Mr. Pruitt over thirty years, but he was easily excited. Later, when David asked his Daddy what the scariest part of that entire ordeal was, he replied, "riding with Willie to the hospital." M. M. Pruitt was called by many their "real John Wayne." David says he came from pretty good, tough "stock."

After earning a BS degree from Texas A & M University and an MS degree in microeconomics at Texas Tech University, David Pruitt learned that, with a recession going on, not many businesses needed his learned college skills, and eventually he took the job that had a company car attached.

David and his wife of two years relocated to Hereford in the panhandle of Texas, where he was employed by an electric cooperative. Deaf Smith Electric Cooperative offered him the opportunity to learn all phases of an electric wires company that would stand him well for his entire career in electric utility work. Later, he served twenty-five years as CEO of two electric cooperatives and one investor-owned electric utility.

As CEO of Cap Rock Electric and Cap Rock Energy for over twenty years, Pruitt initiated business endeavors that had never been tried or achieved in the electric utility business, and as he says, "Some of them even worked." These included but were not limited to guaranteeing continuity of electric services and paying claims on lightning hits (i.e., not blaming God for the lights going out). The culmination of these initiatives was going public (IPO) with the first electric company in sixty-five years and then later taking the public company private—transactions that had the potential of making stockholders nearly $100 million if all had sold at just the right time. Along that journey, Pruitt's company nearly ran out of cash and faced bankruptcy while Pruitt contemplated the possibility of making payroll for over three hundred employees out of his own pocket.

During his life, Pruitt was an entrepreneur doing many things, including owning a chain of weight loss businesses and moonlighting to pay off unsecured debt by doing electrical wiring and selling insurance. He was still ranked in the top fifty producers of a life insurance company even though it had been almost twenty years since he sold his last insurance policy.

David's book of quotes is sprinkled with many of his own and many you may have heard, which he has been collecting for many years. The quotes of David are driven by his experience in business and life and reflect the way he solved the many challenges he faced by being the first to create new solutions. His new and unique solutions to challenges sometimes created jealousy and even fear in others in the electric business, and because of the electric cooperatives' "Good Old Boy System," he took many arrows in his front and back.

David was married to his high school sweetheart, Patricia Ann Pruitt, who died of cancer after thirty-one years of marriage. Not long after her death, a close friend strongly encouraged David to go on a chaperoned, blind date with the friend's cousin. Pruitt was "smitten" right off, and a little over a year later, they married making her married name also Patricia Ann Pruitt. So David has been married to two ladies with the same married name for a total of forty-six years. David said, "You have to cull them deep" to have that outcome.

After he sold his stock in Cap Rock Energy, where he was the largest stockholder, David and Pat have traveled extensively, visiting all the continents of the world and over seventy countries.

David's quotes reflect the many unique experiences he has encountered, such as "After you have children you are never more happy than your saddest child" to "No one ever died from being kicked in the balls."

We hope this will be a fun read; think about what David was going through during the thirty-plus years of his collecting quotes.

CPSIA information can be obtained
at www.ICGtesting.com
Printed in the USA
LVOW01s0429111215
466320LV00020B/447/P

9 781612 542119